THE REVEAL

Bryan has written a readable blueprint for easing into retirement. Uniquely, he has included tips for wrapping up a business, as well as some useful considerations for dealing with personal income tax issues that are relevant to most individuals on the verge of retirement. This is a helpful book that I would recommend to my fellow retirees.

WAYNE BALDWIN, mayor, City of White Rock

THE REVEAL

STEPPING ACROSS THE LINE INTO RETIREMENT

BRYAN SOMMER, CPA, CA, CFP®, CIM

Published by Advantage, Charleston, South Carolina.
Member of Advantage Media Group.

ADVANTAGE is a registered trademark and the Advantage colophon is a trademark of Advantage Media Group, Inc.

Printed in the United States of America.

ISBN: 978-1-59932-744-0
LCCN: 2016954405

Cover design by Katie Biondo.

This publication is designed to provide accurate and authoritative information in regard to the subject matter covered. It is sold with the understanding that the publisher is not engaged in rendering legal, accounting, or other professional services. If legal advice or other expert assistance is required, the services of a competent professional person should be sought.

Advantage Media Group is proud to be a part of the Tree Neutral® program. Tree Neutral offsets the number of trees consumed in the production and printing of this book by taking proactive steps such as planting trees in direct proportion to the number of trees used to print books. To learn more about Tree Neutral, please visit **www.treeneutral.com.**

Advantage Media Group is a publisher of business, self-improvement, and professional development books. We help entrepreneurs, business leaders, and professionals share their Stories, Passion, and Knowledge to help others Learn & Grow. Do you have a manuscript or book idea that you would like us to consider for publishing? Please visit **advantagefamily.com** or call **1.866.775.1696.**

The content of this book is not intended to constitute legal, accounting, financial or tax advice by the author. If you would like personalized financial advice please contact a licenced financial professional in your jurisdiction. The views expressed in this book are the views of the author in his personal capacity.

While I may reference stories about some clients, I have changed their names and a few facts to protect their anonymity or amalgamated some of their experiences to highlight themes we see when working to achieve clients' goals. Reference to any program or course is not intended to be an endorsement of the person offering the program or course or his or her services.

To my clients . . .
for your trust and motivation to exceed expectations.

To my wife and family . . .
for your encouragement and support.

To my father . . .
for your guidance and mentorship as a financial planner.

To my mother . . .
for without you my life would not be possible.

Some say retirement is the reward for a lifetime of effort. But if it is truly a reward, why do so many other people loathe the idea of drawing their working careers to a close and facing the ultimate freedom of retirement?

In my forty years as a chartered professional accountant and investment advisor, I have witnessed even the most confident of individuals confront their pending retirement reality with great trepidation. Over and over again, the biggest concern I hear is whether the new-retirees and their significant others will happily adjust as they stare at each other over their morning cups of coffee.

Fortunately, every retiring person I know has found a new daily ritual with relative ease and comfort. However, lurking in the back of everyone's mind is their own mortality and whether they have the financial resources to provide for a long, cash-flow-deprived future. Regrettably, with age comes unforeseen health issues, and although most of my clients boast healthy, active lifestyles, sadly a few have not bounced back from health issues.

It is this fear of outliving a lifetime's accumulated capital that's driven my business model and financial planning approach. I have focused on alleviating clients' fears by demonstrating to them that managing their personal cash outflows and building a balanced investment portfolio with modest return expectations will, for the majority, provide a worry-free retirement. And in the rare occasion that an unforeseen event causes cash flow concerns for my lower mainland of Vancouver clients, we work together to generate an injection of capital by looking at their whole financial picture, perhaps by downsizing to a more manageable residence.

Ironically, as my own retirement date approaches, I have to acknowledge that I have had some of those same pangs of retirement remorse. I have the added anxiety of ensuring that all of my clients, many of whom have been with me since my public accounting days over sixteen years ago, will continue to be served in a professional, proactive, and thoughtful manner. Finding a successor that has all of these qualities—and a professional accounting designation to carry on the unique delivery and analytic components of my business—has been absolutely essential to me. I feared that finding a candidate with all of these qualities was going to be a very difficult task.

As fate would have it, I did not have to look beyond my own neighbourhood. Financial planner Frank Sommer and his family lived in our neighbourhood in the 1980s. Although Frank, his son Bryan, and the rest of the Sommer family moved after a few years, our relationship was rekindled when my eldest son and Bryan played on the same lacrosse team. I have always firmly believed that being involved in team sports builds leadership skills, and as a gifted lacrosse and rugby player, this became very evident as Bryan matured.

When Bryan later graduated from university and began working as a chartered professional accountant with a local accounting organization, Frank offered Bryan an opportunity to follow in his own footsteps by joining him at his investment management business. As part of Bryan's exploration process, he came to speak to me about the investment industry, its future, and the challenges we faced within our profession. Needless to say, I was impressed with this young man, and after discussing my future plans, I encouraged him to keep in touch.

Bryan *did* keep in touch, and in a little more than five years after our first exploratory meeting, he has become an experienced investment advisor who has developed a deep understanding of our profession and how to service his clients in a very comprehensive goals-focused manner. His commitment to his clients is evident by their trust in both his approach and work ethic. In short, Bryan is an individual who I fully trust to serve my clients and continue my forty-year legacy as I move into my own, worry-free retirement. Those pangs of remorse are long gone.

That is what this book, *The Reveal,* is all about: going into retirement with a plan in place and your eyes wide open. Don't leap into retirement life cold turkey. In my long experience, it's the clients that engage in the financial planning process and understand the risks and returns of their investments that have the most success in living their retirement dreams. They understand the impacts of their changing cash flow needs and its impact on their net worth. Bryan has captured the essentials in the pages that follow, but he's gone a step further—he's given you a roadmap to understanding your retirement choices and how to search out the professional services of a respected, talented investment advisor who will help you to minimize financial uncertainties and provide a path for a healthy and prosperous retirement.

Enjoy the book, but more importantly, enjoy your rewarding years of retirement—you've earned it.

—ALLAN ECCLESTONE, B.COMM, CPA, CA

TABLE OF CONTENTS

FROM CANDY TO BUGATTIS

Standing in front of a class of fourth graders was quite a change of pace for this financial planner and accountant who generally advises older folks preparing for retirement. Here was an opportunity to teach the fundamentals of financial literacy to the playground crowd.

"Who can tell me the difference between a *need* and a *want*?" I asked. I gave a few examples to prime their thinking. "You know, like water is a need, but a milkshake is a want…"

"Candy!" one young man called out. It was a day or two after Halloween, so tricks and treats were top of mind for the majority in this diminutive demographic.

"That's right," I said. "Candy is a good example of a want. It's nice to have it, but you don't need it." Most of the class nodded.

"No, no, no, Mr. Sommer. It's *not* a want," the student interjected. "Candy is *definitely* a need." He was adamant and elaborated at length upon his reasoning. "Candy gives us energy, see? We need energy to live. So we need candy to stay alive."

Most of his classmates again nodded. Opinions, at any age, are so easily swayed.

After my presentation, I offered each student a parting gift. I passed around a bag containing an assortment of candy and pens so that each child could choose one or the other. I noticed that the boy who had insisted that candy was a life essential decided instead on the power of the pen. Who knows? Maybe he planned to use it to advance his cause.

I've been surprised at the level of sophistication that some of these young people express when we talk about money. They're not just learning to count nickels and dimes to save up for bubble gum or a toy. Some aspire to greater heights.

"I want a Bugatti!" one earnest young student exclaimed. Yes, a sports car costing a few million dollars, pricier than most houses. At least he didn't try to persuade the class that it was a need.

Teaching financial literacy is my way of giving back to my profession. CPA Canada, the association of chartered professional accountants, sends volunteers into schools and workplaces to help children and adults alike learn financial skills that so often are lacking. The association recognizes that teachers and parents seldom address the essentials of good money management.

It's a responsibility that I long have taken to heart. I wrote a book for small children a few years ago called *Gifted Goose Learns about Goal Setting* and developed a fun app called Pogo Pig Savings that teaches toddlers the self-control that leads to financial success later in life. And so I was pleased to join CPA Canada's effort. Many of the retirees with whom I work donate their time to worthy causes, sharing their perspectives and wisdom. Younger people should follow their example. Giving back brings balance to our lives. Volunteers are among the healthiest and happiest of souls.

Those bright young people whom I have met as a volunteer have many years ahead of them. Someday they will be bright older people in their fifties and sixties contemplating retirement. They will use those smarts in so many ways to contribute to our society, as entrepreneurs and engineers, as teachers and accountants, as business owners and professionals and community leaders. But when all is said and done, and they are looking to pass the baton to the younger generation, much of their retirement success will come down to the fundamental lesson that I shared with them that day.

The question when they are older will be how well did they define their needs and wants throughout their working years. In other words: Have they lived within their means? Have they earned more than they spent? Have they set aside money for emergencies? Have they saved and invested in anticipation of their retirement—or, in words that a child might better understand, have they saved for a rainy day?

That young man who grabbed the pen instead of candy might not actually have understood which one would ultimately be better for him, but I like to think he made the best choice. I'm all in favour of writing things down, of planning and organizing. After all, I am a financial planner. That's what I do. I help people to make the right choices as they prepare for retirement. Not everyone understands or agrees, at first, what will be good for them, but as we develop a trusting relationship, they come to respect my guidance.

A TRANSFORMATIVE TIME

In my profession, I see life at both ends and in the middle as well. Volunteering in the schools has reminded me of the perspectives of youth and the freshness of starting out and experiencing the world. And as I advise older people and retirees, I often meet their children as we resolve family and estate matters. Many of those younger people are launching their own children into college, filled with dreams and promise, and sometimes I meet those grandchildren to help with educational aid. Some clients want to set up funds for newborns in the family. The concerns of the elders seem to naturally focus on the needs and wants of the children and grandchildren, and, therefore, I find myself of service to all ages.

One recent morning, I heard from the son-in-law of my eldest client, who is 104 years old. She had suffered a serious fall and was in the hospital. It was time to make sure that her affairs were in order. I do see the spectrum of life, with all its wonders and worries. During times of stress, in particular, the support of a trusted professional can make all the difference.

I can tell you that the older set whom I advise on money matters have more than candy and Bugattis on their minds. No matter how much money they have amassed in their working lives, they share what seems to be a primal concern: "Will I have enough?" They want to know whether their savings and investments will be sufficient to maintain their standard of living, whatever that might be. They want assurance, primarily, that they will not run out of money before they run out of life. And by "enough," they also often are wondering whether they have the resources to help out their children and grandchildren along the way or to secure a legacy via philanthropy. They are trying to determine whether they have reached a state of financial security that will expand their options as they enter retirement.

Such uncertainties can derail retirees' expectations, and those unknowns go far beyond how well their investments will perform. One of them is their state of health: Will they be physically able to enjoy these later years and afford medical costs? What about taxes and inflation? Unexpected expenses also can dramatically change the financial plan for retirement. Building a contingency and emergency fund is essential. All of these considerations and contingencies must be addressed. Otherwise, retirees might find their options contracting rather than expanding, and the choices could be unpleasant. Sometimes they feel forced to sell their house to keep up with the bills. Working together, we strive to ensure that doesn't happen.

"Enough" is relative. It depends on lifestyle and expectations. Yes, a few might want their Bugatti, but most people have somewhat less-extravagant tastes. Certainly they should aspire to an income that accomplishes much more than paying the bills. Life is about reaching for dreams—but in reality, many people have not paused along their path to contemplate those lifetime goals. For years they have run in circles pursuing success, but they have yet to define what success is. Now is a perfect time to do so.

Retirement is one of life's transformative times, when it feels as if the rules have changed. During the accumulation years, life was about stocking the storehouse. Now it's time to begin living on those provisions. Doing so effectively requires a new way of thinking and a new way of managing finances.

We live longer these days, and that longevity in itself has revolutionized retirement planning. In 1950, the average length of retirement was eight years. In recent times, it has been more than double that length. That's great news, but it comes with a caveat: today, it is more important than ever that retirees have a secure retirement income that lasts longer than required in the past. That means the focus is no longer on how high a return they can get and how much they can accumulate but rather on how they can protect what they already have. Reducing financial risk is crucial in retirement.

A BALANCED APPROACH

The core of my clientele consists of people nearing or just entering retirement, as well as those who are well along in their later years. They want to make sure that their estate is in order. They generally are age fifty or older, but when I deal with my clients I am also dealing with their families—their children and grandchildren and often their elderly parents as well. We work to address goals that involve all of them. In that way, my office considers our clients to be part of our family because we strive to provide devoted and responsive care.

The pre-retirees with whom I work include business owners and professionals, such as accountants, lawyers, doctors, and engineers. Most are looking to reduce taxes and minimize risk in their portfolios. They tend to have relatively large incomes of $150,000 a year or more, which means they can benefit greatly from the tax management that I can provide. Many of my new clients come to me as referrals from other accountants who recommend my services, as well as from engaged and satisfied long-term clients.

One of the fundamental questions, whether they already have retired or are preparing to do so, is whether they can do something to reduce the tax burden—and the fundamental answer is yes, there are many options. Saving on taxes seems to be a universal desire for people at any level of income. Even if it's protecting only a dollar, people see that savings as a victory. I'm pleased to say that I am able to save them many, many dollars as we put the tax laws to use in their favour. Often, I am able to defer income and flatten the tax brackets to save them a considerable sum. In many cases, this is done working with clients' accountants, incorporating well-thought-out plans with a high level of service. We will take a closer look at tax management in chapter 5.

If someone comes to me who seems merely to be looking for the highest possible return on investment, we must consider whether we would be a good match before we commit to working together. I do assist younger people in the accumulation phase of their lives, but even then it is important to minimize risk. We need a reasonable return, but we are not looking to invest as if we were at a casino. If someone is looking for a consistent 20 percent return I would tell them that it is not possible. We would never guarantee the performance of an investment portfolio.

Still, in those earlier years when people are building their wealth, they do have a longer time horizon. That allows some people to take more risk in the hope of achieving a greater return. Again there is no guarantee that investing in higher risk investments will yield a higher return. From what I have experienced and observed, chasing a hot tip never works. If it seems too good to be true, it often is. Today's latest and greatest will often become tomorrow's poorest. Those who want only to obtain the ultimate return and compare performances and benchmarks are looking for something other than the comprehensive financial planning that this book, and my practice, entails.

What we offer is a balanced approach in line with life goals that produces ample income so that the retiree need not return to work or cut back along the way. The proper investment mix depends on individual circumstances, needs, and goals. What works for my clients are the carefully considered and measured investments that fulfill the retirement goals and the risk tolerances that they have set forth. I work with professional teams to put together investment plans that serve my clients' best interests. We are looking for an overall high rate of success, not a smash hit that would come at great risk with a low level of consistency. We need a relatively high level of consistency with our performance to remain accountable to clients as they pursue their goals.

WHILE THERE'S TIME

Though most of my clients are older, this book will be of value to readers of any age who are interested in preparing for a fruitful retirement—and it is never too early to start. For readers who are within five years of retirement, however, it is particularly important to keep turning these pages. Though they may have done a good job of saving and planning during their accumulation years, they need at least a few years before retirement to make sure that everything is organized properly.

I have found that those five years before retirement are when people are most likely to be taking a close look at where they stand. For years they have been preoccupied by career and family life, juggling their responsibilities, and now that they have come up for air, they see how quickly they are approaching the end of those working years. It is time to critically assess whether their plans are in order and whether they can, in fact, retire.

It's also time to critically assess the advisor. That person might have done a fine job of helping them during their accumulation years, but he or she must also be familiar with the needs of people in the retirement phase of life. The accumulation years are a time for growth and high returns. With so many years stretching ahead before retirement, younger people have time to compensate for a mistake or from losses in a bear market. Time is on their side.

Older people lack that time advantage. As they near retirement, they need to reduce risk, and the advisor must understand that. They should be working with someone who is naturally conservative and will work cooperatively in avoiding the risks that could wreck a retirement plan. Together, they should be striving to create a plan that meets life's goals effectively and efficiently.

It is, of course, essential to produce a rate of return sufficient to keep pace with inflation, and I do seek to outperform the indexes. The return, however, must be appropriate for the client's needs and goals, which become clear to me as I get to know the individual, the couple, or the family. What often happens is people will look at the TSX or the S&P or the Dow, and they will wonder why they haven't been getting such returns themselves. Here's one good reason: they are seventy years old and retired. It is essential at that age to have a portion of income with little risk. The investments might not rise as high as the index on the upside, but they also don't suffer on the downside as much.

Before accepting greater risk, retirees must be sure that they have covered their short-term needs and can project an income that will last a lifetime. They must take a look at the breadth of their retirement expenses, consider how long they might live, and plan accordingly. As long as the appropriate portion of the portfolio remains relatively secure, other parts can take on more risk to enhance the return.

Retirees should have a short-term fund sufficient to sustain them for several months, and they also need money that will be working for them to beat inflation so that their portfolio, too, has greater longevity. I have gotten referrals from accountants who have been working with business owners seeking a better way to invest. Often I find that all of the cash in the corporation is invested in guaranteed investments earning 1.5 percent or sometimes less. They would like their money to work harder for them. Many are at a point where they need a better return with tax efficiency if they want their money to last. Playing it too safe can also put a retirement at risk. Again, this highlights the importance of working with an advisor who fully understands the particulars of the client's situation and aspirations.

IN MY BLOOD

Still in my midthirties, I am quite young compared with most of the other professionals in this industry. The typical advisor is perhaps twenty years older, and though I respect those years of experience, I also know that my clients value my relative youth. They have been looking for someone to manage their money who will still be practicing for many years to come. Retirees with a high net worth want the confidence of continuity as their assets pass from generation to generation, and estate planning is one of the primary services that I provide.

My clients know that I will be there for them, and I will be there for their children and for their grandchildren. I will not be retiring myself just as they are settling into a comfortable retirement. They have seen clearly the importance of building a strong and trusting relationship with a financial advisor, and the last thing they want to do, as they are trying to enjoy their retirement, is to devote their energies to building such a relationship with someone else.

I practice what I preach: even as my wife and I are beginning our family, we are looking years ahead. I'm a family guy. My wife, Justyna, is a naturopathic doctor, and our daughter, Arianna, is a one-year-old. Family issues are high on my own priority list, and I can empathize on those issues when I work with clients, regardless of their age.

I love what I do. I have had many opportunities to pursue other careers, and this is the one that I have chosen. I didn't just stumble upon this path and land here. I actively sought it out as my life's work. Most days I come to my office with a smile on my face, feeling energized at the prospect of meeting with clients and their families and helping them to clarify their goals and their visions and work toward attaining them. In doing that for them, I am doing that for myself and for my own family. In so many ways, I find fulfillment in my career.

As a Chartered Professional Accountant, I am an investment advisor and portfolio manager with CIBC Wood Gundy. I find that my accounting background is particularly valuable to my clients, as I can provide service on tax issues. That remains an unusual skill among the majority of financial planners. I also have attained the designations of CERTIFIED FINANCIAL PLANNER™ and Chartered Investment Manager.

You might say that what I do is in my blood. My father, too, was a financial planner, and I have learned well the lessons ingrained in me as I was growing up. My teenage reading list included such books as *The Wealthy Barber* and *Rich Dad, Poor Dad*. I can tell you that those were not the sort of books my classmates were reading. By virtue of my father's example, I took an early interest in matters of finance and accounting and planning for a productive and fulfilling life.

That, in essence, is what I do for people. That is the passion that drives me. I help them to accomplish their goals, to reach for their dreams. Those goals might be modest or grand, practical or ethereal. I might be involved in funding a grandchild's savings plan or helping a business owner efficiently transition to the next generation. I help my clients to set up an efficient estate plan and to support the charities of their choice. I assist them in organizing their life priorities as they move from their years of accumulating to their years of preserving. Together, we find the best ways to safeguard what they have worked so hard to gather.

This is custom designing. I am not a stockbroker who peddles products at someone's bidding. I am an investment advisor, but I deal with much more than investments. I attend first and foremost to the individual needs of the client and the client's family with a comprehensive range of services, using the financial tools specifically designed for their particular circumstances. The only way I can do that is through developing a relationship with them so that I understand their situation and all the details. Customizing takes time and dedication.

Each of us has a unique combination of goals and dreams and values, and we have differing tolerances for risk. Clients come to me with a portfolio that may or may not be realistic for retirement, and together we must balance their goals and resources until we attain a workable plan. I must pay attention not only to the level of risk with which my clients can feel comfortable but also to the level that their portfolio can tolerate if they are to meet their objectives. I help them to manage those risks, which could continue for three decades or more in retirement. We will be taking a close look at the range of those risks in the chapters ahead.

Throughout this book, I also have included portraits of retired people I have known. I have asked them to share their stories. As you will see, their lives reflect the themes—the victories, the struggles, the dreams—that are familiar to so many people as they transition into the new world of retirement.

IN MY LIFE . . .
FRANK AND SUSAN

Having secured the resources to retire comfortably, Frank and Susan took the big step after they were certain their three children were financially independent. Now their challenge was what to do with so much time.

Frank had begun his career in the insurance business before becoming an investment advisor and financial planner. Later, a son took over the business. Susan had worked as a teacher, flight attendant, real estate agent, florist, and in several other pursuits. A talented painter, she began selling her works. She had already eased into retirement, and so Frank followed suit.

Uneasy, at first, about having so much time off, Frank was soon enjoying a busy but less stressful life. Today, he golfs and plays tennis and badminton, sometimes all three in the same day, while Susan has become an avid cyclist. They enjoy their separate times and also their togetherness. In the past, they could never have considered taking a month off to travel across Canada.

Frank and Susan have long volunteered at the Whistler ski resort, where they met. They relish their time with friends there, and as mountain hosts they get that essential sense of community that retirees so often miss after leaving the workplace. Once, they talked a lot about moving to Whistler, but with their family now spread out from Los Angeles to Melbourne and a new granddaughter in White Rock, they are reassessing their options. In short, they want to be footloose.

It's a common pattern: retirees often downsize not out of necessity but for flexibility. They may wish to live for extended periods in various locales, often for family reasons, and a large house can be a maintenance headache. Some would rather use the equity to gain more freedom.

Frank and Susan are finding that this new chapter of their lives is rewriting itself in exciting ways. They are adjusting well as they embrace life together. And the reason I know so much about them—if it isn't obvious by now—is that they have long been in my life. I call them Mom and Dad.

CHAPTER 1

NEW HORIZONS

I had been dating Justyna for about a year and a half when I knew beyond doubt that it was time to propose. She had been in India several months, introducing a health product into that market in her capacity as a naturopathic doctor.

I had the opportunity to visit her there, and I arranged in advance with her friends and associates who were accompanying her to tell her that they would be doing a video shoot for a commercial in front of the Taj Mahal. I asked Justyna if I might come along to observe and perhaps help out.

The grounds were swarming with tourists, particularly where we were doing the shoot, considered an ideal spot for photography. Nonetheless, her friends cleared the space, set up the equipment, and began the video. And then, just before she began to speak, I stepped forward and took over the show. We recorded it all.

For us, that was one of life's thresholds. We were about to enter a new state of living called matrimony. We married in Tuscany, just outside of Florence, in a castle atop a hill. And on January 8, 2015, we entered yet another phase of life, when

Arianna came into the world. I share those special moments here because I know that each of us can reflect on similar times in life when everything seemed ripe for change, when we were on the cusp of different and better things.

I felt that way, as well, when I started a small business with a friend after studying entrepreneurship at the University of Victoria. It was a clothing-with-a-message company called Navigate Apparel. We created shirts for charity efforts and more, encouraging others to "navigate their lives." One was in support of a fellow rugby player who climbed four mountains in one day in Alberta to raise money for the Canadian Mental Health Association. Another was for the Special Olympics. My friend still operates that business, but for me it was more of a giveback. Mostly what I gained from it was the satisfaction of encouraging others to go after the good things in life. This, too, was about the excitement of launching into something new.

Retirement is another of those transitional times when everything changes. It is a time of full commitment, when you realize there will be no going back. You are crossing the line into new territory. It is exciting, but it can be disconcerting. You feel a deep weight of responsibility, but you willingly take it on. Your thoughts turn toward the future and what you need to be doing so that you and your family will thrive.

These are the perspectives that arise when you marry, when you have a baby, when you start a business, and when you retire. You feel the need to nurture, provide, and protect. For people getting into their fifties and sixties, there comes a time when they realize that they are about to do it again. There's a big change coming, and it is called *retirement.*

WHEN THE PAY CHEQUE STOPS

The retirement that people imagine and the one that they experience can be quite different. This can be a time of surprises—happy ones, we hope, though not always. As they envision the retirement to come, people often see it as a time of relaxation, of sweet visits with the grandkids and long conversations on the porch, of golf and travel and glorious freedom. When they get to retirement, however, they often find that they are as busy as ever—not in a bad way, necessarily, but they have no trouble finding ways to fill their time. They visit and they volunteer and they give back to the community. Sometimes, they also find that they need to go back to work, not because they want to but to balance the budget. It's unfortunate, but it's common—and with proper planning, it can be avoided.

In short, reality may not meet expectations. Retirees need time to adjust. Many people have not really thought about what retirement will be like, other than they no longer will be "working." That well might be a welcome change, but for many people those years of working had much to do with how they defined themselves. Retirement can feel disconcerting, as if they have been stripped of their identity.

"Work gives us structure and meaning in our lives," writes Derek Milne, retired clinical psychologist and author of *The Psychology of Retirement: Coping with the Transition from Work*. "It's hard to predict what kind of changes might unfold." These are normal feelings, and nothing is strange about wanting to go back to work. What is unfortunate is feeling forced to go back to work because of a lack of effective planning.

Those who miss their career often prefer to transition more slowly into retirement. They keep a hand in their profession so that they feel that they still are contributing in a meaningful way. Some of my clients have postponed retirement for that very reason, and some have worked as consultants and started businesses.

Whether they are financially set or not, retirees must be ready for the day when the pay cheque stops. Something must replace that regular compensation from the employer or the business. That stream of income can come from a variety of sources: a company pension, for example, or government benefits, perhaps even a British pension. Primarily, retirement income will flow from investing the savings accumulated over a lifetime. Comprehensive planning can lead to a seamless transition of income in retirement, but those who have done insufficient planning are bound to feel unsettled by the uncertainty of not knowing whether they will have enough.

At the same time that retirees are making this financial adjustment, they also will commonly be facing new challenges in their marriage, and without doubt they will need to make adjustments in this arena as well. I am happy to report that, from what I have observed among my clients, those adjustments usually go well. If both spouses are willing to work together toward common goals, then they find that they can manage their time effectively so that they feel strong as individuals and as a couple.

Marriages, in fact, often improve. Couples are past the stresses of their child-rearing days, and generally the kids are out of the house and on their own. No longer do they need to get up and rush about in the morning. They can keep their own schedule, planning it together, and they can include on that schedule some things that they have long wanted to do but never seemed to have the time. As I see couples work together, I often feel excited for them. It's as if they are dating again. This new spirit of togetherness is particularly likely to grow when couples take the time to consider what is important to each other, a perspective that I encourage as they develop their financial vision. As we work together to reduce the stress in their financial lives, they feel a new sense of freedom. They feel young again.

Retired people, however, by definition are getting older, and they will inevitably face health challenges. I have seen what can happen. Health issues can arise at inconvenient times. One client had a stroke as he and his wife were visiting Palm Springs, and they faced an issue of insurance coverage due to a technicality. Fortunately the client regained his health and they were able to withstand the financial strain of the health-care costs. Such situations underscore the need to anticipate such contingencies. Thorough planning can do much to ease retirees' financial stress regarding health issues, whether they are abroad or at home.

It is wise to prepare for retirement not just in the few years before taking that step but during the decades prior. Developing a mind-set that will serve well in retirement is the way to avoid the unpleasant surprises. If traveling has been a lifelong passion, for example, that spirit will extend naturally into the retirement years. Those who see themselves doing volunteer work during retirement should have a long history, from an early age, of donating their time to the causes they care about. In other words, people should practice the lifestyle that they expect to continue leading. That way, it doesn't seem as if it is all happening at once.

Sometimes people work hard, scarcely giving themselves a break, expecting the big payoff when they finally stop working—and then they don't know how to deal with that time. Might it not be better to level out the leisure and the labour for better balance? Perhaps they could take more time off during their working years and then more gradually ease out of their career, perhaps working part-time until age seventy. For some, that approach provides a less stressful transition. The millennial generation has a penchant for pursuing life balance, and that's a mind-set that people of any age would be wise to adopt. I can see myself easing into retirement that way someday. I love what I do, and as long as I am healthy and able I would want to keep a hand in this profession.

CHANGING PERSPECTIVES

For better or for worse, the contrast between the working years and the retirement years is starkly different, with a new set of worries and concerns.

Many younger people, for example, are focused on starting a family, buying a house, and saving for their children's tuition. They are thinking about advancing their career and getting promotions and raises to keep ahead of inflation. With so much time on their side, they have years before retirement for their fortunes to grow. Younger people are busy spending and accumulating what they can, but retirement must also become a specific financial goal.

Older people who are nearing retirement often find their mind-set changing. As with my parents retiring and downsizing, many couples focus on establishing flexible living arrangements so that they can visit their kids (and grandkids) who have spread their wings across the globe. As these types of new retirees transition into retirement and begin to explore their housing needs, there are other elements they must consider as well. For example, they should choose a place that will benefit them in their retirement—a community that offers near-at-hand medical services and a healthy lifestyle.

Community is more than just a collection of houses and people. It can also set the tone for a lifestyle. A study by Stewart Wolf focused on the small Italian community in Roseto, Pennsylvania, sought to establish a link between the community you live in and your health.[1] As a physician servicing Roseto, Wolf noted that people under the age of sixty-five from Roseto are rarely ever diagnosed with heart disease. After further investigation, he determined that their health was due to the tight-knit, family-focused, and egalitarian nature of the community. Though it's just one study, the "Roseto Effect" underlines the importance of observing a community as a whole when you are considering a living arrangement now or in your retirement. Though Pennsylvania is nice, you may just do what my wife and I did for our wedding and go straight to Italy for your health… and maybe the food and wine.

Italy aside, if people nearing retirement have been planning properly, their focus becomes not so much on growing their money but on preserving it and using it wisely. If they have done a good job of planning, they have paid down all of their debt. They are not facing any immediate large expenses. What they are concerned about now is managing their level of risk during retirement so that they do not run out of money. They seek to decrease their vulnerability in the stock market, keep up

---

1   Malcolm Gladwell, "Outliers: The Story of Success," *New York Times*, Nov. 28, 2008.

with inflation, and control taxes. They are looking for the right balance of income and expenses.

They also want to feel fit and able to enjoy retirement, and they are concerned about the costs of health care. And if one day they might need long-term care, they often want to make sure that they have enough money so that they can choose for themselves the level and quality of care that they will receive. Many of my clients have told me that they want to plan toward getting that choice. They don't want to be left at the bottom of a long waiting list when they need an immediate examination or surgery.

Retirees generally are keenly aware of how they might be blindsided by unexpected expenses. They have lived long enough to understand the importance of an emergency fund. It is particularly important in retirement to set aside a sum of money that is liquid and easily accessible and not invested in anything risky. Ideally, that fund should consist of a year or a year and a half's worth of income. Maintaining such a fund will provide them with options during retirement if the market should drop. The emergency fund can take care of living expenses until the market rebounds. Retirees who are forced to withdraw significantly from their portfolio when their investments are sagging may never recover from their losses. An emergency fund can offset that risk.

As they prepare for retirement, people often express a desire to provide for their children or grandchildren. Much has been written about the "boomerang generation," in which a young person goes off to university and then boomerangs back to live as an adult with Mom and Dad. Today, sometimes it's a double or triple boomerang. It's not easy, right out of university, to get a job that pays well. It's hard to afford a $1 million house—a typical price in Vancouver—on an income of about $50,000.

Some young people think that they straightaway should have what their parents have. They want the lifestyle they have had growing up, but they do not want to wait thirty years to acquire it on their own. There's a disconnect in their thinking. Nonetheless, parents have a natural tendency to want to help their children out. The trick is to do so without spoiling them. As Warren Buffett put it: "I want to give my kids just enough so that they would feel they could do anything but not so much that they would feel like doing nothing."

Many of my clients have enough money to buy their children a car, or even a house, but hesitate to do so. Their own parents generally didn't provide them with such luxuries. They worked for their money, and that is what helped to shape them into who they are today. That is why some clients, in designing their estate plans, do not want to leave their life's work to their children. They do not see that as encouraging independence and success. Rather, they are concerned about dampening their children's motivations and ambitions. As loving parents, they are seeking balance in their children's lives so that they can learn the skills to thrive.

Few parents or grandparents would refuse all help, however, and many do choose to assist the younger generation. Some even budget for it. They might help with a deposit on a house, for example, or they might fund the grandchildren's Registered Education Savings Plans. I understand that desire. Our daughter is the first granddaughter on both sides of the family. We often hear that being a grandparent is better than being a parent. I see the twinkle in our parents' eyes when they see our daughter.

For those who wish to provide financial support, good planning is a must. This should not be an expense that arises suddenly, setting off a scramble. Those children will be growing up for years, and that means their parents and grandparents can put years into figuring out how best to assist with proper boundaries.

How to determine the amount of money needed during retirement is a common question, but the answer has many variables. Financial planners can create models and scenarios and draw up budgets to get as close as possible, but a comprehensive plan must consider the emotional as well as the monetary issues. Many people's retirement plan amounts to: "I have saved this much, and now I will retire, and life will be beautiful." It's not quite that simple. The financial plan must be able to handle a variety of scenarios, some of which can be quite distressing.

A couple may retire, for example, and feel guilty taking regular trips around the world as a son or daughter works two jobs, burnt out from work and family responsibilities. Some people cannot feel good about their retirement unless their kids have reached a certain level of independence as well. Every retiree needs to consider the point at which he or she will step back from being a parent. Perhaps their children will be happy that Mom and Dad are taking that European vacation. Perhaps they won't. It's a concern seldom expressed but often deeply felt. What is the appropriate parenting role? It's all part of the changing perspectives of the retirement years.

GETTING FULLY FUNDED

The two big questions that people must ask themselves in preparing for retirement are these: *How much money will I need?* and *Will I run out of money?*

The rule of thumb that retirement income should be 60–80 percent of pre-retirement income may or may not apply. Those who have been able to eliminate debt may need less income, but others may see expenses rise, particularly in the early years of retirement when they are in good health and eager to travel and pursue other activities. Those expenses tend to decrease in later years.

The joy of dining out tends to be replaced by the joy of home cooking. Then, as health issues arise, expenses tend to rise again. It's a pattern that is typical, and it can be anticipated in the planning.

The other big question is whether the money will last. In his book *Someday Rich*, Tim Noonan, a longtime leader in the private wealth management industry, explores the concept of the funded ratio, which is similar to how a pension company determines whether it has enough money to meet its obligations and fund the payments that it has guaranteed for employees.[2] He suggests that individuals can do the same to predict retirement success. They can examine their assets, liabilities, and cash flow and calculate how close they are to guaranteeing future payments to themselves. In other words, they can determine the percentage by which their future is funded—whether 100 percent or something lesser or greater.

---

2 Timothy Noonan and Matt Smith, *Someday Rich: Planning for Sustainable Tomorrows Today* (New Jersey: Wiley Finance, 2011).

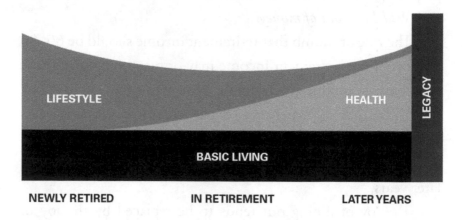

HOW NEEDS CHANGE IN RETIREMENT

LIFESTYLE

HEALTH

LEGACY

BASIC LIVING

NEWLY RETIRED

IN RETIREMENT

LATER YEARS

How needs change for a typical retirement over time.

Once people have reached the point of being about 130 percent funded, they face little likelihood that their ratio will drop to 100 percent funded. It might seem counterintuitive, but they could take on more risk in the market if they so desired. Because their future is secured, they can afford to go after more bang for the buck.

HELP ALONG THE WAY

Adding to the stress of retirement is the fact that many key decisions must be made, some of which are irreversible, such as choosing among pension options. And among those major decisions will be finding a good advisor. That's not something to do on the day of retirement. The advisor will be assisting potentially for decades to come, so that relationship must be comfortable and based on trust.

I recently met with an engineer who had never had an advisor before me. He had been cynical about the value of paying someone for advice. But after I worked with his wife and him and we designed a retirement plan that clearly spelled out the options, I could feel the tension ease in the room. He told me that he had been sceptical before meeting me but that he had come to feel very comfortable. He had come to see the essential role of financial planning.

By carefully weighing the money coming in and the money going out and anticipating future needs and wants, retirees can avoid getting into situations that are financially and emotionally troubling. I never want to see my clients have to sell their house or go back to work just to make ends meet. Both of those should be options done willingly, not out of necessity.

I have seen the range of concerns that people face as they begin the transition into retirement. As they move from the younger years of accumulation to the older years of preservation, strategies must change. This is generally the time to be taking on less risk, although with sufficient return to beat inflation. Retirees should invest differently, and they should be working with an experienced professional who understands why.

CHAPTER 2

DREAMS FULFILLED

A few years ago, when Justyna and I were married in Italy, my father stood up at the reception to relate a story about me. When I was about ten years old, he told our guests, I wrote a list of the fifty things that I most wanted to do in life—and one was to take over his business someday.

Little boys do not tend to aspire to playing with numbers when they grow up, but I admired my dad and wanted to be like him. I still do. I have had a lot of other options in my accounting career, but I know the path that I have chosen is the right fit for me.

I was goal oriented as a kid, and that continued into high school and university. One of my favourite classes in the entrepreneurship business program at the University of Victoria was a career planning course. I created a ten-year plan that established my goals and action steps. Looking back, I see that I got pretty close to the exact career path and the steps that I have taken to getting where I am. The experience of developing that plan inspired me to write a children's book about goal setting.

Several years ago, I did indeed take over my father's practice. He had continued to teach me, as an adult, lessons about life and career. He grew up on an Ontario farm, driving huge combines even when he was a child. He passed on a strong work ethic to his children, encouraging us to strive for the best. I mowed lawns and shovelled snow. I babysat, and I refereed lacrosse. I washed dishes and cooked at a White Rock beach restaurant, and I scrubbed clubs at a golf course. For a few summers I worked as a field hand, tossing and stacking hay bales. It was the kind of tough farm work that my father had done as a boy, and I wanted to feel what it was like.

I'm sure that I must have spent some time goofing off, as well, but for the most part I was a kid with an entrepreneurial spirit. I went door to door in my neighbourhood on my rollerblades, lining up those mowing and shovelling jobs. I also was a kid who was deeply into sports. I had a sport for every season and often two at once. In high school I got an award for playing on the most sports teams, including volleyball, basketball, soccer, rugby, lacrosse, and more. In the world of sports, too, I thrived on the hard work. I saw how healthy competition and teamwork build character. On several of those teams, I also served as captain. I learned about leading by example, and I learned about respect.

A PARENTAL PERSPECTIVE

Justyna and I often are asked why we chose to get married in Italy. Neither of us is Italian. The simple answer is that we both love Italy. Where better to marry than Tuscany? The cuisine and the wine are wonderful. I recall asking a waiter about a pasta entrée. He told me that it had been on that menu and unchanged for half a century, so he could say with confidence that it would be a good choice.

Justyna grew up in Poland, and when she was a little girl she lived with her parents in a dormitory as they attended university. They later moved to Germany for a few years and eventually to Winnipeg—but after just one winter there, they were ready to relocate to the Lower Mainland of British Columbia.

Like me, Justyna had observed her parents working hard, first in their studies and then as they started from scratch in Canada. Her father is a brilliant man who runs a machine shop making specialized parts for just about anything, including airplanes and mining equipment, and even a part that went into space. Justyna's mom is a computer software developer and has created programs for the Safeway grocery chain. She is also the president of the Canadian Polish Congress of BC. Her parents instilled in her a set of morals and values similar to the ones that my parents instilled in me. She excelled in naturopathic school, earning the award for top marks in her graduating class.

Today in her practice, Justyna takes a holistic approach in working with her clients. She knows that she must fully understand them before she can truly help them and offer good advice. In that way, our careers are similar. We do not just treat the symptoms and move on. We care about the whole person. We care about the family. We don't try to solve a problem by prescribing some pill that might present complications elsewhere. To do this right requires a devotion of time and a solid relationship with those we serve. It is true in my career, and it is true in hers.

Justyna is a model mom who is devoted to her new role. I have seen how well she works with children in her practice, and she brings that special touch into our home. We also are lucky to have two sets of grandparents who are able and eager to help out. We feel it is important that she not interrupt her career as a naturopathic doctor, and we are confident that we can raise our children well in a two-career household. It is healthy and sustainable for both parents to develop rewarding careers, but it calls for dedication and a clear delineation of priorities and goals.

Like other parents, we dream about our children's future. It is a centerpiece of our planning, just as it often is a central consideration of my clients. We want Arianna to have options. Someday she may wish to pursue a family tradition of financial planning or of naturopathic healing. We imagine her in those professions, but we know that she should follow her own dreams. In any event, we want her to share our focus on managing health and wealth. We want the best for her.

Life changes when you have children. Priorities change. That has become so clear to me, and that perspective gives me an ever-greater understanding of my clients. We can anticipate how to handle all the big changes in life. It is my privilege to help people find the best path through that transition called *retirement*.

THE FINANCIAL VISION

New parents, if they have a chance to reflect amid the hectic pace, often begin to ask themselves what life is all about and the goals they wish to pursue. As retirement nears, people again tend to look for that big-picture perspective.

In working with my clients, we develop a three-page Financial Vision document (see Appendix I: Financial Vision).

The purpose is to come to a meeting of minds so that I clearly understand their circumstances and can make the appropriate recommendations on their behalf. I am looking for clarity and direction.

First page: What is really important to you?

On the first of three pages, we identify what matters most. That might seem simple, but often when both spouses are together and I ask that question, they look at each other and then back at me. I can tell they haven't talked together about such things in quite some time.

Usually, one spouse or the other is more tuned in to the financial statements and investments, but they must not skip this step. I often find that the spouse who is least interested in the nitty-gritty of the numbers becomes much more engaged at this point. "What do you like doing?" I ask. "What do you want to make sure will be happening now and later on? Let's talk about several things that are really important to you."

After some discussion, we come up with a list. At first, couples tend to talk in generalities, such as wanting to have consistent cash flow in retirement. But those numbers eventually evolve into some specifics: "We've always wanted to go to Peru and hike the Machu Picchu Trail," for example. I often hear the words "golfing" and "gardening" and "traveling." I hear a variety of topics that are not necessarily related directly to money.

This is all part of my effort to reach a greater understanding of my clients. Only when I can think like them will I be able to advise them well. Later, as we work toward specific objectives and goals, I will be able to make sure that we sacrifice nothing important as we set priorities. Having a list helps both my clients and me to maintain the right perspective when we get down to the details. They sometimes seem baffled at why I am asking such questions, as if to say, "Well, sure, we can talk about this stuff, but here are my statements and when can we start talking about the numbers?" Rest assured, we will.

This is a step that grows trust. When both spouses observe that we regularly review and update these fundamentals at virtually every meeting, they come to see the depth of caring that I bring to our relationship. They see that all decisions will be based firmly on what matters most to them. We spend plenty of time on the numbers—and with my accounting background, I tend to enjoy numbers more than most—but in doing so, we don't neglect the dreams.

I created the first page of the Financial Vision document based on my training in the High-Speed Strategic Planning program of consultant Steve Moore, a former coach with the Seattle Seahawks, Buffalo Bills, and Los Angeles Rams who now focuses on helping businesses achieve their goals. He understands that to attain powerful numbers, you must first step back from them.

Second page: Where are you today?

I based the second page of the Financial Vision document on the gap analysis of the Pareto Systems training program. In effect, the focus of this page is: "Where are you today?" This page functions as a dashboard so that I quickly can see whether anything is out of whack. If that appears to be the case, then we will go deeper. Otherwise, we can see at a glance whether the client's situation is functional.

This is quite a timesaver. Clients often have told me, "A financial services professional did this free financial plan for me, but it took a long time, and all those questions were exhausting. And then they gave me thirty pages that were so detailed that I didn't want to read the thing." I see a disconnect there. The people who create such documents are not speaking the same language as the client. Sure, the details are important, and personally I enjoy the numbers. I have found, however, that many of my clients don't. What they want and need, up front, is simplicity and clarity. In this shorter, more dynamic statement, we can see right away whether we are on track and how we might need to adjust.

Page two looks at four categories: cash reserves, debt, growth/income, and insurance. For each, we take a look at both the current status and the expectations for the future. If the right trajectory doesn't seem to be there, then we delve deeper to find the alignment.

In examining the cash reserves, we find out how much is in the client's chequing account and the amount of daily expenses. I sometimes find that older clients have accumulated so much with their company pension and Canadian Pension Plan (CPP) and Old Age Security (OAS) that they wouldn't be spending it in five years. Sometimes, that's the way they want it—they sleep better knowing that money is available, and they are reaching their goals without it. When that's the case, then we leave it be. Often, however, we decide together to put the money to work for them. In other scenarios, clients have very little money in their chequing account and would like to have more of a buffer. We may decide to begin building an emergency fund so that the client feels more comfortable.

In the debt category, we determine how much clients owe and how they want to deal with it. Few people want to remain in debt, and so we set expectations. For example, some clients may wish to continue carrying a mortgage, with the goal of downsizing to a less expensive house in three years. Once we have the objective, then we can set the course to get there.

We also look at the growth and income from investments. What is the anticipated income level? Are the investments accomplishing that goal?

And finally, we take a look at insurance coverage. We make sure that it is appropriate for the client's current situation. Sometimes, we find a real need, particularly coverage in the event of a premature death. But we might also find that the client is carrying unnecessary insurance. The mortgage and debt have been paid down, the kids are out of the house—so what is the point of keeping that term insurance? I have often observed that people buy insurance and then neglect to review their ongoing need for it. I help them to do that. Yes, the offer might be a good deal—but nothing is a good deal if it is not needed. The insurance salesman might know that a policy has good terms but not whether those terms fit the customer's situation.

SENSIBLE INSURANCE

People often ask me whether their insurance coverage makes sense for them. The only way to know is to fully understand their situation—and seldom does a salesman take that time. Here's an overview of typical uses for an insurance policy.

Generally, insurance is best used to cover an expensive but unlikely occurrence—for example, the death of a healthy, middle-aged person who was the household's main income earner. If that person were to die, however slim the chance, he or she might be leaving a house with major debt and a spouse with kids to raise and little earning power. Term life insurance can protect the family during the period when the death of the breadwinner would be financially disruptive.

Insurance also is a valuable tool for covering a specific tax liability. Let's say you have a ski chalet that you want to become a family heirloom. However, your children might someday be forced to sell it if they cannot pay the taxes after you and your spouse pass away. To prevent that, you could buy a permanent life insurance policy to cover that obligation.

An insurance annuity to produce a guaranteed income stream is also popular at times, although not with the recent low interest rates. Some people also use universal life insurance policies as another method of deferring taxes. In addition, it can be used to create a tax-efficient estate, and in a corporation, an insurance policy can fund a buy–sell agreement between partners in the event that one of them dies.

Although cost prohibitive in some cases, disability and critical illness insurance can also be an effective solution to bridge the gap in many people's health insurance coverage.

As you can see, insurance has a wide variety of legitimate uses. It is a powerful tool—but like any tool, it must serve the right purpose or it could be useless, or worse.

Third page: Your planning objectives

On the third page of the Financial Vision document, we drill down to the main objectives that require time, money, and planning to accomplish. We strive to identify up to three key ones, to which we usually estimate the expense and set an expected date to achieve them. Then we can set priorities for which objectives will get top attention. This creates a sense of accountability. Sharing an objective can be quite motivating. You're not just telling yourself, "This is one of my goals, and maybe next New Year's I'll think about it again." When you know that someone will be checking in on you, you're more likely to take that goal seriously.

Above all, I like to know why the objectives are important to the client. That helps me link the objectives back to the first page of the Financial Vision document—the fundamentals of why we are doing this. When we keep getting back to that *why*, the priorities make more sense. I get a feel for the extent of enthusiasm that clients bring to their stated objectives. I can tell whether they are approaching them out of a sense of obligation or out of a sense of excitement, and that alone speaks volumes about the proper priority. Sometimes, what is exciting should be first in line, and other times we need to make sure the enthusiasm for one goal doesn't drown out the importance of the others.

GOALS-BASED REPORTING

In conjunction with the Financial Vision document, I use a graph called "Goals-Based Reporting" that provides a measure of accomplishment. You can find this in Appendix II: Goals-Based

Reporting. First developed by Steve Moore and Tim Noonan for a Russell Investments High-Speed Strategic Planning course, the graph is a way to interpret the returns over a specific period in light of the goals that a client has established. In other words, if the market drops 3 percent, what does that mean for the individual's portfolio and bottom line? Clients tend to be most concerned with the bottom line.

The goals-based reporting graph shows how a particular change to the financial plan will influence the achievement of an objective. For example, if $50,000 were added or subtracted, how might that affect the timing of when a goal would be achieved? We can project whether a change would still result in success.

Again, a major benefit from this is accountability. We are able to see consequences clearly. We can see the real effects of market fluctuations. A $10,000 decline in a portfolio, for example, might not chart out to significantly alter the financial goals as a whole.

As the market moves up and down, people tend to count the percentages. We help them to see whether those percentages count as part of the big picture. We interpret whether they are still on track according to their plan and whether we should make any adjustments.

A ROADMAP TO CONFIDENCE

Sound financial planning starts with the big picture. It is important to see the pattern of the puzzle before trying to fit the pieces into place. It is a reverse engineering approach that identifies the design before the details.

When done well, financial planning instils confidence. That can only happen when the plan is tailored to the individual. My clients do not get a plan off the rack. Instead, I tailor a plan designed exclusively for them. Once they can see how they will accomplish their unique objectives, the weight of worry lifts. They can feel more lighthearted about life.

There is risk in not knowing financial situations. Whether retirees have more money or less money than they imagined, they need to become fully aware of that amount. When people's dreams are far out of line with the size of their portfolio, trouble lies ahead. It can go either way: Some retirees have extravagant visions of travel and luxury that the portfolio cannot support, and others have multimillions and yet live in fear of running out.

Failure to prioritize can wreck a retirement. I have seen parents with such slavish devotion to their kids, wanting them to have it all, that they consider downsizing their house and liquidating investments. Parental pride is laudable but not to the point of getting so carried away that retirement dreams dissolve. Most people will have multiple goals, but they must understand that if they overindulge in one, they could be sacrificing others. Spending lavishly today on family vacations might have a ripple effect that means doing less in retirement.

This need not be a guessing game: through goals-based reporting, we can project the outcome. What most people want to find is the right balance, and that starts with identifying goals early and abiding by a plan.

I also have encountered couples who simply don't realize that they are financially in good shape. They come to me in fear of running out of money. That attitude was even more common among survivors of the Great Depression and those who lived through the World War II years. They were in save mode for years and actually were becoming quite wealthy—but they had been so conditioned to frugality that they scrimped, even in retirement.

I still see couples like that. They are making more than they are likely to spend, sometimes just on pensions, let alone their own investments. They could be doing so much more. They could be vacationing with family or helping a great-grandchild with university expenses. Rather than leaving a huge lump sum someday, they could be experiencing more of life now. Often, their children and grandchildren encourage them to enjoy themselves more. Once again, seeing the big picture provides the benefit of clarity: retirees might be able to adjust their spending upward, not necessarily downward, to meet the realities.

I have seen those two types of disconnect, and both are sad. Some people throw all of their resources into living for today. They might feel they have good reason, but they are sacrificing the quality of their own retirement. Other people pass up opportunities to enjoy life. Rather than living for today, they are always fretting about tomorrow. Certainly we all need to plan for tomorrow, but we need not live in fear. We can live in clarity and confidence.

How do we get there? I use what I call a roadmap, and it's another of the core planning documents that I find valuable in working with clients. The roadmap consists of agendas that we set up for the next few years, the topics of discussion that we will broach, and our implementation plan to bring the financial vision to fruition. I want to make sure that we don't miss anything and that my clients know that there will be a time and place to thoroughly discuss everything of importance. You can find this roadmap in Appendix III: Roadmap.

This is a way that they can hold me accountable to dealing efficiently with everything that we decided together to include in their plan. Instead of overwhelming my clients with a thirty-page financial plan, I serve all the information to them in bite-size pieces.

IN MY LIFE . . .
LOIS AND GERRY

Retired for ten years, Lois and Gerry have this advice for younger people: travel as much as you can, while you are able to make the kind of memories that might be more difficult to accomplish when you get older. Balance savings, investment, travel, and work. Manage your money so you can live more comfortably in your retirement years. Save with Registered Retirement Saving Plans (RRSP) and Tax-Free Saving Accounts (TFSA), and invest wisely and maintain a goal to pay down your mortgage over time. Without debt, your retirement years are easier. Make a plan and live within your means because your years pass quickly, and suddenly you are sixty-five. Ask yourself what you want your financial picture to look like and make it happen.

As snowbirds, Lois and Gerry live in California during the winters and come home to British Columbia for the summers. Golf and travel remains important to both of them—but they point out that trekking through a jungle is an endeavour more suited to a younger soul. They are more likely today to take an excursion to a Hawaiian beach or visit their daughter who lives in France than to be hacking through the tropical undergrowth.

Lois balances her own schedule and activities with the time she spends looking after her widowed mother who, along with her two sisters, ensure that their ninety-six-year-old mother is cared for properly. Like many baby boomers with aging parents, Lois has taken on the responsibility of handling her mother's finances. She finds a team approach that incorporates her financial advisor works best.

They underscore the importance of health, family, and travel—a theme that is nearly universal among retirees—and they emphasize the importance of pushing your comfort zone and enjoying a wide range of life experiences. Memories matter, they say. If you don't create them when you are younger, you cannot buy them later.

A SYSTEM OF PRIORITIES

With a strong system, ordinary people can accomplish extraordinary things consistently. That's how franchises thrive. They offer a system for success that if followed faithfully will produce results.

My system of the Financial Vision gives me a strong in-depth knowledge of my clients. We can see clearly whether everything is in sync, ensure that we are covering all elements of importance, and remain accountable to the established goals. That's what we aim to accomplish through the goals-based reporting and developing the roadmap. The system also includes an asset allocation questionnaire that helps us to ensure that the portfolio mix is aligned with those goals and needs.

The process arises from the vision. If we only look at rates of return from year to year, or year to date, we cannot necessarily see the progress. The performance results can change dramatically just by altering the dates even by a week. Goals-based reporting, by contrast, examines whether the investments are positioned to accomplish what matters most to the client. Meanwhile, the roadmap ensures that we are addressing, in logical order, each of those important matters. All this is done in conjunction with the asset allocation step.

I cannot overemphasize the importance of finding priorities in life. The kind of questions people should be asking themselves throughout their lives, and particularly during the transition into retirement, include these: *What do I hope to accomplish? What will make me feel happy and fulfilled? What will I do with my money? Do I have a "bucket list"? Will I leave anything to charities, my family, or both—and what is the right balance? What is my purpose here on earth, what is my "why," and how do I want to be remembered? What do I want my legacy to be?*

Those are the questions that build the framework upon which we can hang the details of a comprehensive financial plan. These are whole-life questions that encompass more than the financial realm. The happiest retirees are those who have a grip on those themes and have set clear priorities. That is why I place such emphasis upon them. True financial planning requires that holistic approach, where client and advisor hold each other accountable.

CHAPTER 3

TRUSTING THE QUARTERBACK

Tom, a longtime client, often would come in to see me, but he didn't much care to talk about details. We would review his investments and other information, but he preferred to chat about fishing and camping. Over the years, I encouraged him to bring his wife, Sarah, to the meetings.

"Sarah? No, she doesn't need to be here," he told me. "She hates investments. She'd rather just keep money in her chequing account. Her idea of investments is Guaranteed Investment Certificates (GIC) at zero risk." Sarah never came along with him, despite my urging. Tom explained that they kept their financial lives separate. He wasn't opposed to bringing her along, but he didn't feel that it mattered.

After a while, I started getting phone calls from Sarah asking where their assets were located. And one day, when Tom came to see me, he was not alone. Sarah was assisting him, guiding his wheelchair. She decided to stay for the meeting, and I soon observed that she was much more aware than Tom of the details. She might not have had an interest in investing, but she understandably had an interest in what was going on with their money.

We took a good look at everything, and we were able to go quite a bit deeper into their financial life. We examined the ownership of assets—some were solely in Tom's name—and we got into the details of estate planning. Fortunately, we were able to make adjustments to save on probate costs. We were able to put assets in joint name in a way that reduced estate costs without triggering taxes.

To get their full financial picture, I clearly needed both Tom and Sarah's involvement. Sarah was much more risk averse than her husband when it came to the market, but investments were only part of what we needed to consider. When Sarah finally came aboard, the additional financial planning was able to save them quite a bit of money and time.

When working with a couple, I need both perspectives. We don't necessarily have to talk about the numbers for the whole meeting. I like to talk about sports and traveling as much as anyone, and those are the conversations that build bonds of friendship. But I do need to make sure that the couple's finances are in alignment with the future that they have envisioned.

Each spouse will have much to contribute. It's about a lot more than money. We need to talk about organizing the estate. What are the family issues that must be resolved for a smooth transition of assets to the next generation? Who will take care of what and when? Worrying about all those details and paperwork, and figuring out how to get access to assets, is not something anyone wants to do when they are in their eighties and their loved one has just passed away. Planning prevents headaches.

No financial planner is a mind reader. There are things that I cannot know unless the client tells me, and that is why I encourage openness and engagement. I'm not saying that people are hiding anything; sometimes, even important information just doesn't come to mind. It's not at the forefront of their thoughts, and they might not particularly like talking about such matters. I guide my clients through a structured process that helps them bring to light anything that would help in designing their financial plan for life.

EVERYWHERE AN OPINION

Not all of the people who walk through my office door know the exact details of what they need. The conversations often start out with broad strokes—"I want to know if I can retire," or, "I want to pay less in taxes," or, "Do I have enough to last throughout retirement?" As I get to know them, I narrow the conversation down to the specifics and begin to look for solutions.

They can feel confident that they have taken the right step. I can assure them that the advice I offer will be in their best interest. Our incentives are in alignment: the more I can help them to thrive and meet their goals, the more both of us will benefit from our long-term relationship. I make my living by charging a percentage of total assets managed. If the client's asset base is down, so is my fee. My clients and I are, therefore, aligned in our interest to grow the client's assets. That is not necessarily the case when dealing with commission-based advisors or stockbrokers, who make money on the buying and the selling, whether the client gains or not. There are good stockbrokers, certainly, but investors always should be aware of the incentives involved.

Investors must be aware, as well, of the incentives that drive media coverage of financial issues. Remember that the media make their money on advertising, and they are producing information for the masses. None of those commentators, whether in print, broadcast, or online, know anything about the individual. One size does not fit all. Everyone has different needs, and the media are not in the business of customizing. Good advice for one person can be dreadful advice for another.

We are in an age when information is everywhere. It can be overwhelming. As my father used to say: "There's so much information out there, it's like drinking water from a fire hose." It's not just the media: friends and associates often boast about their financial prowess, with much to say about where the smart money should go. They say little, of course, about their setbacks. Either way, they are living their own lives with their own needs and goals and circumstances. The forty-year-old who is holding court at the water cooler has different priorities than the sixty-two-year-old and the twenty-four-year-old colleagues who are getting the earful.

How, then, can anyone glean good advice from such an avalanche of ideas? Start by cutting out the irrelevant information that aims to elicit an emotional reaction. There is much of that in news coverage, so be wary of that source. We need to get down to the core facts that can help us make sound decisions.

When I arrive at my office in the morning, I usually have dozens of emails that include analyst reports, changes in bank rate decisions, economic outlooks, and much more—all of it focused information that is devoid of emotion and relevant. But even among those, I have to pick and choose from reports coming from an array of investment management companies. It would be impossible for me to read it all, but I need to be confident that between my team and I, we have absorbed enough from credible sources that my decisions will be based on reliable information.

My role as an investment advisor and a portfolio manager is to gather and sort through the details and apply them in individual ways that best serve my clients. I know which information merits the most attention and which can be set aside. Do-it-yourself investors, unless they are highly experienced and engaged, are at risk of getting sidetracked amid the swirl of data and reports. It's a big job that calls for full-time attention. For most people, an ideal retirement doesn't involve hours of concentration in front of a computer screen.

I do work with some clients who enjoy keeping a close watch on their investments, and they tend also to be the ones who take the reins on all aspects of their financial life. They watch the markets closely, but they also understand that they can't do it all themselves and need guidance in structuring and adjusting a portfolio. Ninety percent of a portfolio's return stems from proper asset allocation, and that is one of the areas where my clients greatly benefit from my services. Those who do enjoy the nitty-gritty of investing nonetheless will do well to have a good team to help them. They will assure themselves of getting more reliable information, and the accountability will help to prevent emotional, knee-jerk decisions often encouraged by news headlines.

A MATTER OF TEAMWORK

I had the privilege recently of attending a seminar conducted by Brian Tracy, a native of Vancouver who is widely known as a specialist in the training and development of individuals and organizations. This is a man with an abundance of energy who has served as a coach to countless people—and yet he surrounds himself with his own coaches. He realizes that virtually every aspect of his life can be improved by consulting with someone who can bring to him an objective perspective and hold him accountable. In thousands of speaking engagements, he has emphasized that coaching brings results, and he demonstrates that in his own life.

That coaching role is an essential element of my relationship with clients. I am there to help them stay true to the decisions they have made and the goals they are pursuing. I am there to help guide them to success, as they have defined it. My clients expect me to hold them accountable and to show the results. In a sense, I am the quarterback as well as the coach, in that I know the plays and do my utmost to execute the best strategy for the situation.

This is a matter of teamwork. Growing up, I played almost every sport under the sun—other than hockey, which might seem odd for a Canadian kid to miss. I played football for several years, taking on the roles of quarterback and team captain. In rugby, I played fly-half and full-back. I learned that success requires the coordination of a variety of people and close attention to the field of play. Each player depends on the others.

An effective financial planning team will include other professionals, including lawyers and accountants—and, with an accounting background myself, I am in a good position to make the right calls. I can bring aboard the best people because I speak the language. The client benefits from both the technical knowledge and personal relationship. In dealing with tax and estate matters, I often work closely with an accountant and lawyer to bring them up to speed with the particulars of my client's situation. Other professionals who might get involved include business brokers, business valuators, real estate agents, mortgage brokers, private bankers, institutional investment managers, estate planners, and insurance agents. We are a team, working together for a win.

Ultimately, the client is, of course, in charge of the team. He or she is getting an abundance of expertise from the specialists, and as the financial planner it is my responsibility to coordinate them. In no way, however, does the client lose control. It comes down to trust. Business owners who are accustomed to being the boss and making all the decisions are likely to feel uncomfortable unless they have built a trusting relationship with their financial planner. My job is to present the options along with the pros and cons. I can recommend a course of action, but the client calls the shots. Armed with knowledge, he or she is able to make an informed decision.

This is much like the way a CEO delegates responsibility to key managers who have expertise in various areas of the business. Those managers report back to the CEO, who is able to focus on the big picture and goals. Business people who have been accustomed to delegating and teamwork are likely to adjust more readily. I have found that engineers implicitly understand the importance of delegation. They tend to be brilliant people, but they also know the parameters of their expertise and how to consult with specialists in other areas. By contrast, small-business owners who for years have worn many hats often have more reservations about giving anyone else a role in their financial life. It often takes longer to form a trusting relationship with business owners, but significant value can be added to their busy lives when it happens.

IN MY LIFE . . .
JOANE AND DAVID

A few years ago, Joane and David decided to sell some of their rental real estate—which freed up time and resources to allow them to travel the world and enjoy cruises. When I spoke to them, they had just returned from the sunshine of the Dominican Republic. Next year they plan to visit Peru and follow the Machu Picchu Trail, and then it's off to Ecuador and the Galapagos. They recently bought a lakefront cottage in the Caribou and are fixing that up as a summer getaway. They enjoy camping and exploring by motor home.

It's quite a contrast to their pre-retirement lifestyle, in which they were busy managing the properties, dealing with tenants and repairs throughout the year. And when they are not traveling—which they do three or more times per year—Joane and David settle in for life at their homestead, where they collect the eggs from their chicken coop and enjoy the songbirds and koi fish. They volunteer at the local bowling alley and at the Bible for Missions Thrift Store.

Life has not always gone so smoothly. Joane was widowed when her husband, a builder, died at age forty-eight in a fall from a roof. She was left with five rental properties to manage on her own. Buckling down, she created a detailed five-year plan, saving and tracking her monthly income and expenses. She scrimped and saved toward her goal of retiring at age fifty-five. When she met David, they joined forces to build their perfect retirement together.

Joane recommends getting an early start to planning for retirement, putting pen to paper and tracking to ensure that it happens. A good advisor, she says, is essential. It is still important to track expenses and set goals in retirement, of course. The end result, she says, is evident in the kind of lifestyle that she and David now are leading—enjoying life and free from the pressure of deadlines and many of the daily demands of the workaday world.

FINDING A GOOD ADVISOR

With so much at stake, what is the best way to find an advisor whom you can trust in a relationship that might continue for decades? You need to feel comfortable talking about the details of your life, and so your advisor not only should be highly qualified but also someone you will genuinely like to work with.

A good place to start is to seek referrals from friends, relatives, or associates who know the advisor well and have used his or her services. Remember, however, that you have specific needs, and the services that pleased your friend might not serve you well at all. You can learn whether the advisor treats clients professionally and cordially, but also make sure that he or she will take the time to assess your situation. If you are heading into retirement, be certain that the advisor has experience with the requirements and concerns of that stage of life.

Your accountant also might provide an excellent referral. Accountants have a lot of information about their clients and generally are quite competent. Those with the Chartered Professional Accountant (CPA) designation are among the top in their field, with particular expertise in tax and business planning.

A reliable standard is the CERTIFIED FINANCIAL PLANNER™ (CFP®) designation, which requires extensive study and examinations. Chartered Investment Managers (CIM) and Chartered Financial Analysts (CFA) also have shown proficiency in portfolio construction and management, which are crucial skills for helping people transition effectively into retirement.

EXAMINING CORE BELIEFS

It can be hard, when working on their own, for amateur investors to avoid making decisions based on gut feelings. When the market is down, the natural tendency is to want to sell and move to cash, sitting tight for a while. Later, after the market has been soaring, they want to get back in. In other words, they sell at the bottom and buy at the top—not a very good formula for growing wealth. I do get phone calls occasionally when the market is down from clients wondering whether they should sell. Several months later, they can see clearly why we left the money alone and what would have happened if we had bailed out. They usually don't call the next time the market is down.

This is human nature, and sometimes the best way for investors to keep a cool head is to consult with someone trustworthy to talk them down from the edge. Technical and quantitative analysis can sometimes predict the behaviour of the markets, but it is the behaviour of the human psyche that has much to do with whether a portfolio will succeed. When emotions get into the mix, people make bad decisions based on fear or greed.

Early attitudes about money, instilled in childhood, lead people to choices that may or may not be wise. Those deeply ingrained attitudes can hold them back or propel them forward in their financial life. When some people think of a highly affluent person, for example, they imagine someone who has cheated the system. Others think of a philanthropist. Those who believe that wealthy people are a blessing to their community are far more likely to become wealthy themselves.

Each of us would do well to examine those motivations within. I can help people see reason in their financial decisions, but sometimes the best avenue to success is to examine core beliefs about money and wealth. It has been observed that people tend to attain about the same level of success as their parents, and that well may be attributable to the value systems they share. We should strive to overcome any quirks in those values that might hold us back and to hold fast to those values that bring out the best in us. If we do not fulfill our potential, we are doing ourselves—and the world—a disservice.

WEIGHING THE RISKS

"How are we going to stop from drowning to death?" a client called me recently to ask. "We need to deal with this!"

From his unusual sense of urgency, I was pretty sure the client was having a gut reaction to the recent news headlines. Yes, the Toronto Stock Exchange (TSX) was down nearly 13 percent over the previous three months, and I could understand why this conservative investor was so concerned.

Knowing we were not subject to the returns of the TSX, I reviewed his portfolio to double check exactly what was happening with his bottom line. Over that same period, his performance was actually up slightly. That seemed to be in alignment with his goal of protecting against risk and drops in the market. His investment mix, designed to meet his stated goals, meant that he would not experience all of the losses of a down market or all of the gains of a rising one.

When the markets are volatile, it's part of my job to have these discussions. I find myself frequently talking to clients about what they have heard or read in the news and how that relates to the specifics of their own financial plan. Or perhaps they got an email from a friend with some red-hot investment tip or about opportunities in micro-trading. I narrow the discussion to this question: "How does that really affect your own situation, and what we are looking to accomplish here?"

Anyone investing in equities can expect some degree of volatility. There will be ups and downs over time, and the performance of an individual portfolio reflects the amount of exposure and risk that the investor has decided to accept for a certain amount of reward. There will be down periods, inevitably, but the perspective needs to be based on a much bigger picture than the daily news reports. The portfolio mix will perform, over time, according to its design.

After I reassured the client who called me that day, he later sent me an email. He had determined, by adjusting the dates, that his portfolio was actually down 5 percent for the specific period that he was examining, by taking the exact highest point in the market compared to the lowest point. He had actually searched for negative news, for the worst possible drop that he could calculate. He could just as easily have discerned the positive: a somewhat different time frame showed a gain of nearly 2 percent. If he had set the dates back another year, he would have seen a 4 percent gain each year, which was right in line with our projection.

I fully understand investors' caution, and I welcome the opportunity to provide perspective. We must be wary of that numbers game. What matters is whether the portfolio is performing over time to meet the established goals of a comprehensive financial plan. A prevailing attitude of negativity can cloud people's judgment. It can lead them to make rash and dangerous investment decisions.

There are many financial risks out there, as we will examine in this chapter. Prospective retirees face the erosion of inflation, for example, and the risk of fluctuating interest rates. They also must consider the fees, some of them not so obvious, that they are paying on certain investments. And what of taxes? Improperly managed, they can be a major portfolio drain. We will examine that particular threat in the next chapter.

Beyond those risks to their wealth, retirees also must consider health issues and the potential costs of special care, or, conversely, the very likely possibility that their portfolio might need to continue supporting them, year after year, into a healthy and active old age.

The risks are many, but they can be anticipated and managed—and one of those threats to a successful retirement is human nature. People need to keep their cool in any economy, and those who seek qualified guidance have the best chance of staying on course. The worst thing they could do is to sell in a panic at the bottom of the market. It is essential to stay on track, emotionally as well as financially, and that begins with establishing clear expectations.

I manage risks. It is a fundamental role as I look out for the financial well-being of my clients. Since most people equate risk with what the market might do to a portfolio, let's begin with a closer look at what is at stake in the world of investments.

MARKET RISK

Retirees must never discount the danger that the market could pose to a portfolio. In the accumulation years of life, when people are contributing regularly to their investments, the volatility is not such a big deal. They have years to go before they withdraw that money, and market dips are actually an opportunity to buy equities at a bargain.

That scenario changes dramatically upon retirement, when the withdrawals begin. If the market drops, say 20 percent, then the portfolio will need to gain 25 percent to get back to even. If the retiree is also withdrawing money from the account at the same time that it is being beaten down by the market, the portfolio will have a difficult time ever recovering. If that is the scenario at the outset of the retirement years, then the prospects of maintaining the desired lifestyle could look bleak.

Some would argue that volatility isn't necessarily a bad thing, because it can create opportunities to buy equities when the market is low and significantly enhance the growth of wealth on the rebound. Then, as the market ascends to a peak, investors ideally can sell at a tidy profit and use the proceeds to look for more opportunities to ride those waves. The key word there is *ideally*, because, so often, they don't. Many do just the opposite. The real risk lies in a lack of understanding of just how volatile a portfolio might be. The investor must proceed in full knowledge not only of the gains that might be expected but of the losses as well.

The time horizon is a critical consideration. The owner of a portfolio might suddenly decide that he wants liquidity—to buy a dream cottage by the lake, perhaps—and that certainly could be arranged by selling the investments and transferring the funds after a three-day settlement period to a bank account. It's a major risk, however, if those funds were being invested for the medium or long term and this transaction was not planned well in advance. If the market is down, that liquidity could come at a big loss. Such withdrawals must be timed to the investor's benefit.

There must be no question about the acceptable level of volatility, the time horizon for the invested funds, and the asset allocation within the portfolio that will meet the client's objectives. That is why I put so much emphasis on developing the financial vision, with the asset allocation questionnaire and the roadmap. Only then can we put together an investment mix that matches the client's circumstances and follow up and track the performance via our goals-based reporting. The client gets the strongest return for the level of risk that is appropriate to the stated goals and timelines.

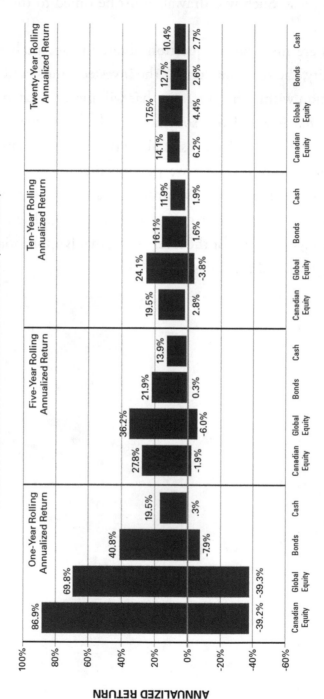

EQUITIES ARE BEST OVER THE LONG TERM
WORST AND BEST ANNUALIZED RETURNS (1950-2015)

One-Year Rolling Annualized Return

	Canadian Equity	Global Equity	Bonds	Cash
Best	86.9%	69.8%	40.8%	19.5%
Worst	-39.2%	-39.3%	-7.9%	.3%

Five-Year Rolling Annualized Return

	Canadian Equity	Global Equity	Bonds	Cash
Best	27.8%	36.2%	21.9%	13.9%
Worst	-1.9%	-6.0%	0.3%	

Ten-Year Rolling Annualized Return

	Canadian Equity	Global Equity	Bonds	Cash
Best	19.5%	24.1%	16.1%	11.9%
Worst	2.8%	-3.8%	1.6%	1.9%

Twenty-Year Rolling Annualized Return

	Canadian Equity	Global Equity	Bonds	Cash
Best	14.1%	17.5%	12.7%	10.4%
Worst	6.2%	4.4%	2.6%	2.7%

ANNUALIZED RETURN

Source: CIBC Asset Management, Bloomberg, as of December 31, 2015

The higher the return that the client needs or wants, the more volatility the portfolio is likely to exhibit. That is measured by what is known as *standard deviation*. Basically, that is the investment's performance above or below the average return over a period of time. A volatile stock will have a high standard deviation. As the investor seeks a higher level of return, the volatility tends to go up exponentially. The shorter the time horizon, the lower the likelihood of actually obtaining that high return from an aggressive portfolio because the range of returns significantly increases. The longer the time horizon, the greater the likelihood of achieving a higher annualized return, and the range of returns significantly decreases.

The length of time in the market, not the timing of it, is what brings success. When investors set long-term financial goals, with assets appropriately allocated, they are more likely to reach their goals. Trying to time the market may block their progress. Investors should not alter their long-term approach based on short-term market movements.

Investors who diversify can achieve a higher rate of return for the risk taken on. The portfolio, for example, might have an asset allocation with a certain percentage of equities, bonds, and cash. As conditions change, the portfolio manager might choose to adjust the positions in a "tactical tilt" to take advantage of areas of higher growth potential. The goal of these carefully considered shifts is to enhance the amount of return for the associated level of risk.

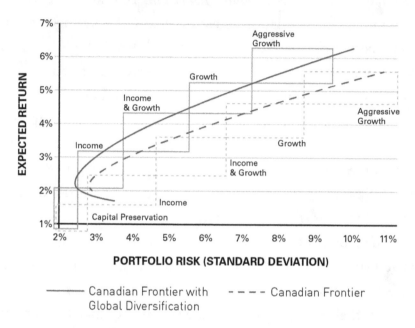

EFFICIENT FRONTIER
(2016 FORWARD-LOOKING ESTIMATES)

——— Canadian Frontier with
Global Diversification

– – – – Canadian Frontier

Risk-return tradeoff showing the importance of global diversification.

Source: CIBC Asset Management

The concept of "efficient frontier" is an industry standard for determining which combination of assets (i.e., the portfolio) has the best possible expected return given its level of risk. The frontier is plotted on a graph, in which one axis is the investment's expected return and the other axis is the standard deviation, which is the measure of portfolio risk. The results reveal the potential return—the "frontier"—that investors might expect based on the volatility they experience. The graph charts the optimal return and thereby shows whether a particular investment mix is efficient compared to that.

Investors can see whether they are taking on too much risk for what they are gaining or whether they could get a better return for the same amount of risk. Generally, diversifying globally will provide a higher rate of return for the amount of risk taken on over a period of time.

Although not specified on the Efficient Frontier chart, the time horizon is extremely important, as noted previously. Depending on your asset mix, the return can vary widely, but if you invest over a period of time, the results are likely to become more consistent and reliable over a longer period, especially for more volatile investments. Generally, the more equity you have in your portfolio, the longer your time horizon should be and the more volatility you should be able to tolerate (see *Equities Are Best Over The Long Term* chart on page 64).

Of all the factors that contribute to the success of a portfolio, asset allocation has been shown to be the single most important over the long term. The various combinations of stocks, bonds, cash, and other assets will produce differing patterns of risk and return. Individual investors must find the appropriate allocation to meet their long-term financial goals. They must find the right balance between return and risk and then stay the course despite the fluctuations of the market.

To stay in line with their original objectives, investors must regularly rebalance the percentage of the asset classes in their portfolios. Statistics show that doing so will enhance the overall performance. A fundamental guideline for your most suitable asset allocation is often touted as the "Rule of 100," which suggests that the percentage of cash and fixed income in a portfolio should be about the same percentage as the investor's age, and the remainder should be in equities. That might work for some as a generally safe rule. At least it demonstrates the broad principle that most people should invest more conservatively as they get older.

However, the Rule of 100 is a one-size-fits-all prescription. People have different goals and, therefore, differing investment needs. Some twenty-five-year-olds might not want 75 percent of their money in equities, particularly if they are saving for a house or other shorter-term goal. And some seventy-five-year-olds might want considerably more than 25 percent of their money in equities, particularly when they have plenty of resources, their spending has dropped off, and they no longer have those shorter-term goals. A qualified advisor who understands the investor's needs and objectives, and the timeline for accomplishing them, can help to design a portfolio that gets the best return for the appropriate risk.

Regular rebalancing of a portfolio is necessary because the asset mix will change over time, simply because some investments will outperform others and thereby begin to take on a greater share of the total. Unless that is remedied, the portfolio will drift away from the long-term asset mix that originally was targeted. When that happens, the investor may be taking on more risk than anticipated. Rebalancing brings the portfolio back into alignment by selling some of the winners and buying more of the assets that have not performed as well.

How often should that be done? If the rebalancing is too frequent, the investor may face greater transaction costs and tax consequences. One study found that rebalancing annually provides the best results. Semi-annual and quarterly rebalancing resulted in slightly lower volatility and returns, with significantly higher turnover. Rebalancing when an asset class was 20 percent off its targeted weighting also produced good results under certain conditions.

Again, this should be done with the guidance of an experienced advisor who will help to keep clients accountable to the goals they have set. Investors may not be naturally inclined to trim a stock that they really like and that has done well, in favour of assets that have lagged. Nonetheless, rebalancing is crucial for long-term success. It helps to lock in gains and control risk.

INFLATION AND INTEREST-RATE RISK

I have not heard as much discussion lately about the loss of purchasing power during retirement, although it does still come up from time to time. Over the last twenty years, inflation has averaged 1.86 percent, compared with the past century's historical average of about 3 percent.

Nonetheless, inflation takes its relentless toll, eating away year after year on the returns in a portfolio. In times of high inflation, even investments that are performing vigorously are hard-pressed to keep up with inflation. In times of low inflation, however, portfolios still need a return better than the rates offered by fixed income and guaranteed investments, which tend to be low as well. Investors make no progress unless the return trumps the inflation rate. They actually lose purchasing power when the return is less than the inflation rate. In today's environment, investors in guaranteed products have a chance to keep up with inflation but likely are not going to beat it, especially in after-tax dollars. To get ahead, they require strategies in which their money can work a bit harder and smarter.

"Our lifestyle hasn't changed a lot," a retired couple recently told me, "but it just seems everything has gotten so expensive out there." They have good investments and good pensions and their CPP/OAS is working for them, but they have noticed the change. Over the years, even low inflation reveals itself. At the historical average of 3 percent, a $1,000 expense today will cost more than twice that in twenty-five years. Retirees on fixed incomes feel the loss of purchasing power more keenly, and some categories of inflation are particularly hard on older people, especially non-discretionary items, such as food, household items, and property taxes.

Many retirees who had anticipated funding their retirement on the once-attractive rates on fixed-income investments have come to see what interest-rate risk can do to their lifestyle. In 1990, they could have invested in GICs for a return of perhaps 10 percent. On a million dollars, that's $100,000 a year. In 2016, on a return of perhaps 1.5 percent, they would get $15,000 a year from that million-dollar investment. As a result, many people have been coming to me looking for ways that they might get a better return, but they need to be cautious as they turn to the markets. It should go without saying that market risk is entirely different than GIC investing, particularly over the short term.

Interest-rate risk often is associated with bond investments. When interest rates go up, the prices of bonds will fall as investors look for greater gain elsewhere. As interest rates fall, by contrast, existing bonds become more attractive because of their fixed rate and gain in value. Because of that seesaw relationship between rates and prices, bond investors face the prospect of damage from rising interest rates.

INVESTMENT FEES

Much has been happening in our industry regarding investment fees. For example, even though explanations of certain fees have been included in the prospectus of a mutual fund, the information is not very transparent. Not too many people actually read all the details of the prospectus.

New regulations require that all adviser fees be included on the investment statement. The intent is to make them so obvious that investors can make no mistake about what they are paying. This has been a trend around the world, and it has raised concerns as investors wonder what kind of advice they are getting for their money.

Good investment advice certainly can produce returns that outweigh the amount paid in fees to compensate the advisor. The caveat is to make sure that those fees are reasonable. Investors must be sure that they are not locked into their investments and there are no penalties to get out. If an investor is paying fees to an advisor but not having at least annual conversations, that might not be money well spent.

To address that concern, I provide annual management fee summaries to our clients. This ensures that we are fully transparent and provides tax efficiency because fees from a nonregistered account are tax-deductible. I also have a list of wealth management services that I provide clients, showing the breakdown of our services and fees showing them what they are paying for. These are in the areas of retirement and tax planning (generally, about 40 percent of the advice given), investment management (30 percent), communications and support (15 percent), and administration (15 percent). I also provide a written fee schedule for family services under management.

IN MY LIFE . . .
JOE AND JULIE

Joe and Julie have found retirement to be a time of unexpected obligations, which they willingly embrace. Their daughter recently was widowed, with two-year-old twins to raise—and so the couple have taken them all in so that their daughter can continue to work.

They had not imagined that as a retired couple in their seventies that they would be looking after a set of high-energy twins. It's a responsibility that tests their own energy levels, but as they have forged a strong relationship with their grandkids, they wouldn't have it any other way.

Joe has been retired for nine years from his job with a company for which he set up exhibit displays. And though their new responsibilities keep them busy, he and Julie find time to enjoy traveling, including trips to see a ninety-year-old sister in China. With so much to do, they understand the importance of a consistent income, maintaining good health, and keeping their minds active.

Joe recommends that younger people work and save while they have the opportunity. He recalls managing employees who refused to accept overtime during busy periods and then were out of luck, with no savings, when the work wasn't available. He emphasizes the importance of spending responsibly. He sees many people who aren't sure whether they can make it financially—and certainly, CPP and OAS alone are not sufficient for most. Even those who think they have plenty should be cautious, he says, and not spend their money too early—particularly not before they even get it.

When he turned fifteen, Joe left school and embarked on a lifetime of hard work. He grew up in New Zealand and spent time visiting family in Hong Kong, where he met Julie. They settled in Canada, where her father lived. They may have survived—but times have changed, Joe points out. Today, their focus is on ensuring that they can help the grandchildren to stay in school, go to university, learn a skill, and get a good job where they can use their heads to make money. He wants them to know the importance of keeping an active mind and constantly learning—and those, likewise, are crucial for a fulfilling retirement.

Julie's father, too, recently has needed extra help, and they were there for him until they needed to switch focus to their daughter and grandchildren. Her father has been able to hire live-in care. Their plentiful travel dreams have taken a backseat, for now, to the obligations that have come their way, although they were planning an excursion for later in the year. They are returning for a visit to Hong Kong.

HEALTH AND LONG-TERM CARE RISK

The wealth risk from declining health and the need for long-term care are not the biggest issues in Canada, where we have a reasonably good health program. For many, the bigger issue is the potential for delays in care. Waiting lists at times can be quite long. If you want a cancer screening, for example, you will not necessarily be walking into the clinic that day to ease your worries. People who can afford to pay more for private care can gain flexibility, with top-notch service that is more timely.

To ensure eligibility for subsidized long-term care, there are ways to structure income and manage taxes. Some people decide to gift funds away so that income is not attributed to them. Once they are eligible for support and their income is low enough, they will have a significant amount of their costs covered if a doctor certifies the need for assisted living. They get put on a list to await an opening in the region, which can be fairly long, and they will get the first room that comes up. That might not be their preference, and they could be farther from loved ones than they would like.

In other words, choices are limited for those who cannot pay additional money out of pocket. Some clients want to make sure that if the need arises, they will be in a nice facility that is close to family, and they save and invest toward that possibility. For them, it is a matter of peace of mind. They want additional options in the event that they are unable to take care of themselves.

What it comes down to is that as we live longer, thanks to medical advances, we face an increased financial risk from that longevity. Decades ago, when people typically lived only a few years into retirement, financial planning was an entirely different conversation. Today, retirees must come to terms with the increasing risk that they might outlive their money.

I recently was working with a prospective retiree on his company Registered Retirement Savings Plan, which projected the payments that he would get in retirement and for how long. Those projections did not anticipate that he would have a long life. They took him to eighty-two years old, a typical age at which a male dies, but most people these days expect to live longer. For my clients, I take the age projection to age ninety at the very least. Undoubtedly, centenarians will become more common. No one should worry about running out of money.

THE RISK OF HUMAN NATURE

Markets, inflation, interest rates, health issues, taxes—all of those and more can get in the way of a prosperous retirement if managed improperly. Let us not forget, however, that one of the greatest risks that people face is themselves. Human nature is not always compatible with wise financial planning. Investors fall victim to their own greed, fears, biases, and faulty philosophies.

A recent Vanguard Group study concluded that, over time, advisors help their clients add three percentage points to their returns. Several factors explain that benefit, including tax and fee management and rebalancing and withdrawal strategies, but fully half of that gain derives from the advisor's role as behavioural coach. They hold clients accountable by keeping them focused on the long term and faithful to a regular investing plan. A good advisor steers clients away from the temptation to time the market and chase returns.

Investors must remember that excitement is their enemy, according to investment guru Warren Buffett, "and if they insist on trying to time their participation in equities, they should try to be fearful when others are greedy and greedy when others are fearful."

Above all, successful financial planning requires self-awareness: What are you hoping to accomplish? What are your motivations? Are you able to rise above emotions to keep a level head with your investments?

CHAPTER 5

TAX SAVVY

The lake cottage that my good friend's grandmother owned in BC had been in the family for years, but the time had come for her to sell. There was no doubt that the cottage had gained considerably in value, so she was working with her accountant to get the preliminary figures on how much she might owe.

As she talked with her family about her plans, however, we begin to consider another possibility. Canada Revenue Agency (CRA) regulations provide a tax exemption on the gain of a principal residence, and in my friend's grandmother's case both her house and the cottage qualified. They were in two separate towns, but both were in her name, and they met the definition of principal residence under tax law.

It quickly became apparent that we needed to find out which of those properties had gained the most in value. If the cottage had gained more, then it might be worth applying some of those principal residence exemption years to the sale of the cottage.

There was another wrinkle, however. Tax law ordinarily allows the exemption on the value of no more than a quarter-acre of a property. If a property is ten acres, for example, only that small portion can be exempted. That limitation generally prevents people from taking advantage of the regulation to realize huge tax savings. Therefore, it seemed we needed to compare the gain on her home to the gain on only a small portion of her lakefront cottage acreage.

When we looked deeper into the tax law with the accountant, however, we found an exception to that limitation: if the owner needs more than a quarter-acre for the personal use and enjoyment of the property, then the entire value potentially can be exempted. For example, if the only access to a cottage is a long driveway that winds up to it, then the entire property is required for the owner's use and enjoyment. We established clearly that such was the case for my friend's grandmother's cottage—the driveway crossed most of the land to get to the lakeside—and as a result she saved tens of thousands of dollars in taxes. The purpose of this book is, of course, not to provide tax advice as you should be consulting with a tax professional but rather to illustrate the value an advisor can bring if they are able to spot issues and bring in the right partner to help you manage all aspects of your financial well-being.

She was advised by her accountant that because of the nature of her use of the cottage. It was not a rental property for which she was getting an income, and she didn't own it in a corporation. It was there solely for her enjoyment during summers, and she lived in her house the rest of the year. As she got older, she found that her trips to the lake country were less frequent, and as a family they thought it might be a good time to sell the cottage. And as it turned out, she was able to do so free of taxes. This was not going to happen automatically, however. It required an understanding and application of CRA provisions and working with a good accountant to execute it.

I share that experience here because I know that it will strike a chord with a lot of my clients and the readers of this book. As I write this, I already have had two clients just in the last week tell me that they are ready to put a property on the market. I recently have been hearing comments such as: "Real estate prices are through the roof here—we're going to sell." They usually find a buyer within a week or so.

The average house price in my town is getting close to $1 million, one of the highest in the Lower Mainland of Vancouver and considerably higher than typical prices across much of Canada. The South Surrey and White Rock area was long a summer escape for Vancouver residents. It's a beautiful region, right on the water, with a touch less rain and more sunshine. My pilot friends call it "the hole in the sky."

A lot of my clients lately have been looking to downsize, so the tax issues that could arise with the sale of a property are top of mind for many. They want to know how best to manage the various considerations and to make sure that they are proceeding in the most efficient manner.

I do have an accounting and tax planning background that is quite unusual in the financial planning industry, and that can be quite a bonus to those clients. That is not to say that my clients should not have an accountant as well to keep on top of all the tax rules and rates that are changing regularly. Accountants have an intimate understanding of the numbers. It becomes a powerful combination of services when I am able to communicate with the accountant and coordinate the planning so that it fits well with the overall strategy. Because I thoroughly understand my clients' overall needs and goals, I can offer perspective on the detailed services that the accountant provides for them. I am not seeking to interfere with the relationship between my clients and their accountants—I am seeking to enhance it.

To save on taxes requires highly customized strategies that take into consideration the client's unique circumstances. Working together, the accountant and investment manager can identify and execute opportunities that might otherwise be missed. With a view of the big picture, they can find ways to adjust or split income levels and reduce the marginal tax rates. With slight adjustments to income, I have seen clients save more than 9 percent instantly.

TAX STATUS OF INVESTMENTS

It is important to understand the significance of the three basic categories of taxable, tax-deferred, and tax-free investments and the role that they play in portfolio management. When each is properly positioned in a portfolio and appropriately utilized, the client can realize considerable savings.

Taxable, or nonregistered, investments are those in which the tax on income will be due in the current year. A wide variety of investments can be included in a taxable account, including individual stocks, bonds, mutual funds, hedge funds, separately managed accounts, GICs, and money market investments. They could be in a personal account, a joint tenants with right of survivorship (JTWROS), a trust account, or a business account.

Tax-deferred and tax-free (registered) investing generally refers to money set aside in a RRSP or a TFSA. Two other tax-deferred accounts include RESPs (Registered Education Savings Plan), for educational savings, and RDSPs (Registered Disability Savings Plan), for people with severe disabilities.

TFSA vs. RRSP

	TFSA	RRSP
Contributions	Contributions are not tax-deductible.	Contributions are tax-deductible.
Withdrawals	Withdrawals are not included in income and, therefore, are tax-free.	Withdrawals are included in income and fully taxable in the year received.
Contributions Limits	2009–2012: $5,000 each year 2013–2014: $5,500 each year 2015: $10,000 2016: $5,500 The annual contribution limit will be indexed to inflation and rounded to the nearest $500 on a yearly basis.	Contribution limits are based on your previous year's earned income up to a maximum amount, less any applicable pension adjustment.
Minimum Age Requirement	The minimum age to open a TFSA is eighteen.	There is no minimum age requirement to open an RRSP.
Maximum Age Restriction	There is no maximum age restriction.	RRSP accounts must be closed by December 31 of the year an individual turns seventy-one.

The assests of both a TFSA and RRSP grow on a tax-free basis. It may be more beneficial to use your RRSP in high-income years since you will receive a tax credit, especially if you will be in a lower marginal tax bracket when you make withdrawals. Both are great tools investors can use in meeting their long-term savings goals.

With the RRSP, investors get a tax deduction on the amounts contributed (which reduces taxable income by the amount contributed), and later they pay the full tax on it when they take the money out. That can be beneficial if the tax rates are the same or lower at the time of withdrawal. With the TFSA, the investor gets no refund on the amounts contributed, but the withdrawals are free of tax. That is particularly beneficial to retirees if their tax rates have risen at the time of withdrawal.

These accounts can be passed on efficiently to successors, particularly if the beneficiary is a spouse. Canadian tax law generally gives spouses the most favourable treatment. The deceased spouse's entire TFSA will be transferred to the other's name, all tax-free, creating a "super-sized" TFSA if they are named as the successor. Similarly, with an RRSP, or in a Registered Retirement Income Fund (RRIF), the money goes into the spouse's account and remains tax-deferred until withdrawal, if they are named as the beneficiary.

For nonregistered plans, couples can set up a joint tenant account with right of survivorship. That way, upon the death of one spouse, the account passes automatically to the other, which is a good way to avoid probate if set up properly. It makes the estate planning easier. The account is in the surviving spouse's name, and he or she has immediate access without having to take the longer, frustrating route as executor. If there are a lot of beneficiaries—a number of adult children, for example—then everyone needs to be on the same page, and perhaps all of them should be added as joint owners. Another option would be to set up a trust.

Still, the joint tenant account is an efficient and simple way to pass assets and avoid probate without the expense of setting up a trust. That's not to say that trusts are not an effective and important instrument in estate planning. For example, money placed in trust is protected from inheritance claims ordinarily permitted under the Wills, Estates and Succession Act in British Columbia. Unlike the provisions of a will, the provisions of a trust cannot be challenged. We manage a number of trusts, and they can be a very effective tool.

TAX-SAVING STRATEGIES

Tax regulations can be quite complicated, but amid that complexity are many opportunities to save money by applying provisions of the CRA code. Let's take a closer look at some of the ways that taxpayers can keep more money in their pockets.

OAS Clawback

Avoiding the Old Age Security clawback is a matter of importance to many of my clients. As I write this in 2016, the maximum OAS benefit upon turning sixty-five is $573.37 a month, depending upon the length of Canadian residency. However, once annual income rises above $73,756 (2016), the government claws back fifteen cents of the benefit for every additional dollar earned, all the way up to $119,512 (2016) where OAS is fully clawed back. I work with clients to defer income or to split income between spouses to avoid the clawback. TFSAs can also be useful for reducing clawback. The OAS benefit certainly isn't enough to fund a retirement, but people still don't like having it taken away. Planning well in advance is the best way to avoid that.[3]

---

3 Jim Yih, "Minimizing Old Age Security Clawback," Retire Happy.ca (http://retire-happy.ca/minimizing-old-age-security-clawback/).

Pension Income Tax Credit

Even though the annual amount you can save from the pension income tax credit is not that significant, it is worth pursuing because it adds up over time.

If you are aged sixty-five and do not have a company pension, you can move a portion of your tax-deferred Registered Retirement Savings Plan (RRSP) into a Registered Retirement Income Fund (RRIF). Then you and your spouse each can withdraw $2,000 a year, and you get a pension income tax credit that wipes away most of the amount that would have been owed in taxes.

Although the tax savings are minimal, a good reason to take this credit is that every year you will be pulling a bit of money out of your tax-deferred account. If instead you waited until age seventy-two, when you're forced to make RRSP withdrawals, then you would be paying full taxes on it. The credit allows you and your spouse several years of tax-preferred withdrawals, and the savings add up.

Income Splitting

Income splitting provides significant tax savings. In retirement, up to half of eligible company pension income can be split between husband and wife. If certain conditions are met, you can also elect to split your CPP and RRIF with your spouse. Business owners have a lot of other options to split income, which we will discuss in chapter 7.

These arrangements can be quite advantageous. For example, a spousal RRSP arrangement allows one spouse to contribute on behalf of the other. The contributor, usually the one in the highest tax bracket, gets a tax deduction. After three calendar years of no further contributions, the lower income spouse then can withdraw the money and pay tax at their lower marginal tax rate. This can be a great strategy if the couple plans far enough ahead. For example, if they know that one of them will not have an income at a certain point, they can start to take money out, and depending on the amount withdrawn it will be tax-free or at a very low rate. This can only work well, however, if they plan early and clearly understand their future situation.

RRSPs and TFSAs

RRSP contributions can be a good way for people with a high income to defer taxes. However, it is important to understand that the government requires minimum withdrawals starting at age seventy-two, and that money will be taxed—and the withdrawal could force them into a higher bracket. For that reason, people may be better off using a TFSA. For example, it may not make sense to contribute to your RRSP and claim the deduction in a low income year where your marginal tax bracket is 20.1 percent, when you know you will be in a high marginal tax bracket of say 47.7 percent when you withdraw it in retirement.

TFSAs are underutilized. A lot of younger investors use RRSPs to get a tax refund on the amount of their contribution. They currently can contribute 18 percent of their earned income, to a maximum of about $25,370 (in 2016), and only if they top that out do they consider a TFSA.

The TFSA, available since 2009 for Canadians age eighteen or over, is a quite powerful savings vehicle, and it can be particularly valuable to business owners who can control income levels. The 2016 contribution limit is $5,500 for each spouse, and the couple can carry forward any unused amount from previous years. For couples who have never opened a TFSA, each spouse can contribute $46,500 (as of 2016). That's a total of $93,000 that they can set aside for retirement without paying tax on the capital gains or on dividends and interest. In a way, that is similar to the principal residence exemption, in which the property gains value over the years, but no capital gains tax is due upon its sale.

Business owners have the option of setting up a corporate investment account instead of using their RRSP or TFSA, which is often a good move; however, it depends on their specific circumstance.

Marginal Tax Rate

In working with my clients, we seek to control income levels to stay within the lower marginal tax rates as much as possible. It is important to understand that greater incomes will be subjected to taxation in a higher bracket. In some cases, it makes more sense to pay taxes now, as long as your income can remain in a lower tax bracket, rather than to defer those taxes until the point when you must withdraw the money, when you might be in a much higher bracket. (The highest tax bracket in British Columbia for 2016 is 47.7 percent on over $200,000 of taxable income.)

By adjusting the income levels, through tax strategies such as income splitting, the savings can be significant. Again, I have seen clients save 9 percent or more. Not a bad return—and certainly not an easy guarantee to get in the market today.

BC PERSONAL TAX RATE TABLE

Federal and Provincial Marginal Tax Rates for British Columbia

2016 Taxable Income	$11,474 to $38,210	$38,211 to $45,282	$45,283 to $76,421	$76,422 to $87,741	$87,742 to $90,563	$90,564 to $106,543	$106,544 to $140,388	$140,389 to $200,000	over $200,000
Salary	20.1%	22.7%	28.2%	31.0%	32.8%	38.3%	40.7%	43.7%	47.7%
Interest	20.1%	22.7%	28.2%	31.0%	32.8%	38.3%	40.7%	43.7%	47.7%
GRIP Div. *	0.0%	0.0%	4.4%	8.3%	10.8%	18.3%	21.6%	25.8%	31.3%
Reg. Div.**	8.3%	11.4%	17.8%	21.1%	23.2%	29.6%	32.4%	35.9%	40.6%
Capital Gains	10.0%	11.4%	14.1%	15.5%	16.4%	19.2%	20.4%	21.9%	23.9%

2015 Taxable Income	$11,328 to $37,869	$37,870 to $44,701	$44,702 to $75,740	$75,741 to $86,958	$86,959 to $89,401	$89,402 to $105,592	$105,593 to $138,586	$138,587 to $151,050	over $151,050
Salary	20.1%	22.7%	29.7%	32.5%	34.3%	38.3%	40.7%	43.7%	45.8%
Interest	20.1%	22.7%	29.7%	32.5%	34.3%	38.3%	40.7%	43.7%	45.8%
GRIP Div. *	0.0%	0.0%	6.5%	10.3%	12.8%	18.3%	21.6%	25.8%	28.7%
Reg. Div.**	7.6%	10.7%	19.0%	22.3%	24.4%	29.1%	32.0%	35.5%	38.0%
Capital Gains	10.0%	11.4%	14.9%	16.3%	17.2%	19.2%	20.4%	21.9%	22.9%

2014 Taxable Income	$11,138 to $37,606	$37,607 to $43,953	$43,954 to $75,213	$75,214 to $86,354	$86,355 to $87,907	$87,908 to $104,858	$104,859 to $136,270	$136,271 to $150,000	over $150,000
Salary	20.1%	22.7%	29.7%	32.5%	34.3%	38.3%	40.7%	43.7%	45.8%
Interest	20.1%	22.7%	29.7%	32.5%	34.3%	38.3%	40.7%	43.7%	45.8%
GRIP Div. *	0.0%	0.0%	6.5%	10.3%	12.8%	18.3%	21.6%	25.8%	28.7%
Reg. Div.**	7.6%	10.7%	19.0%	22.3%	24.4%	29.1%	32.0%	35.5%	38.0%
Capital Gains	10.0%	11.4%	14.9%	16.3%	17.2%	19.2%	20.4%	21.9%	22.9%

2013 Taxable Income	$11,038 to $37,568	$37,569 to $43,561	$43,562 to $75,138	$75,139 to $86,268	$86,269 to $87,123	$87,124 to $104,754	$104,755 to $135,054	over $135,054	
Salary	20.1%	22.7%	29.7%	32.5%	34.3%	38.3%	40.7%	43.7%	
Interest	20.1%	22.7%	29.7%	32.5%	34.3%	38.3%	40.7%	43.7%	
GRIP Div. *	0.0%	0.0%	6.5%	10.3%	12.8%	18.3%	21.6%	25.8%	
Reg. Div.**	4.2%	7.5%	16.2%	19.7%	22.0%	27.0%	30.0%	33.7%	
Capital Gains	10.0%	11.4%	14.9%	16.3%	17.2%	19.2%	20.4%	21.9%	

* The rates indicated apply to dividends received from a taxable Canadian Corporation where the dividends are eligible for the enhanced dividend tax credit.
** The rates indicated apply to dividends received from a taxable Canadian Corporation.   Last updated January 10, 2016

FALLING THROUGH THE CRACKS

A business owner recently informed me that he had learned that his friend, a bookkeeper who had been preparing his tax returns for years, had not been taking full advantage of income-splitting opportunities. The business owner had been doing what he does best—running his business—and delegated the tax management. But as a result, he had paid thousands of dollars unnecessarily in taxes. The lesson is clear: thorough planning pays dividends. It is important to have a good team working together to address issues early and accurately.

Inadequate planning does not necessarily result in some major blow. More typically, the loss results from money falling through the cracks, year after year. Missed opportunities can add up significantly as time goes by. In the previous chapter, we looked at an array of risks that people face as they plan their retirement—and the failure to appropriately manage taxes must be considered high on that list. A good tax advisor will help to ensure proper deductions and strategies. And on the flipside, the advisor can help to prevent improper deductions. People who do their own taxes and misunderstand the rules easily can get into trouble and face penalties and interest. Professional assistance can help to audit-proof the tax return.

As with all aspects of financial planning, the best tax strategy depends upon the individual client's needs, goals, and circumstances, and nobody can truly provide comprehensive advice without thoroughly understanding those particulars. The expertise of a lawyer and an accountant is crucial, along with an investment advisor and financial planner to coordinate all of the professionals on the team.

The goal of tax management is not to deprive the government, but to present and file in the most efficient manner possible and claim what is rightfully yours. This is not tax evasion. This is tax smarts. The tax regulations include numerous legitimate means by which people can reduce their obligations. Those rules are in place for good reason: to promote saving for retirement, for example, or for education or to encourage donations to charity. Tax breaks provide incentives.

It is up to you, however, to figure out the best strategies to pursue and the appropriate deductions. Some are relatively simple, and others are quite complicated, and it is beyond the scope of this book to explain them all. In appendix IV, I have included an assortment of tax tips as presented by Jamie Golombek, managing director of tax and estate planning for CIBC Wealth Advisory Services.

Nobody from the CRA will be knocking on your door to explain those tips or how you can cut back on what you send to the government. Nor is it likely that you will get any tax advice from stockbrokers—that's not their focus. You can either research it all yourself, if you are so inclined, or you can engage the services of a professional accountant who can point the way to significant savings.

CHAPTER 6

ENOUGH FOR A LIFETIME

"I would like all the single people here today to stand up," the seminar speaker announced to the crowded auditorium. "Here's your chance to meet people of a similar mind-set." With my best posture, I stood up, I scanned the audience, and I noticed across the room a young woman who also was scanning the room. Our eyes locked.

It was a three-day self-development seminar that my brother had persuaded me to attend. The program was a powerful experience, with ten-hour days and a variety of speakers. The seminar got participants to think deeply about what might be helping them or holding them back from attracting and managing money properly.

"You are the root of your financial success or failure," the speaker explained. "If you work on the roots, the 'fruits' will take care of themselves." The seminar inspired me to participate for more than two years in monthly self-development course work.

I had met the woman across the room briefly on the first day of the seminar. She was a friend of a friend of my brother and his wife. And then, on the third day of the seminar, the thousand attendees were divided into groups according to their money personalities—that is, whether they were spenders, savers, avoiders, or "money monks." The first two categories are obvious; the latter two describe people who dislike dealing with money and those who feel that amassing money is a spiritual wrong. I was pleased to find that we both were in the saver category.

We started chatting, and we hit it off. It was a month before we went out on a date, though—and Justyna still teases me that it took four dates before I kissed her. I guess I was just being conservative, which is natural for an accountant. Of course, it all worked out. Today we are husband and wife and the parents of our one-year-old daughter.

I'm grateful that we met the way we did and that we took the time to get to know each other. That seminar was a perfect opportunity for me to meet a woman interested in learning and developing herself, who also feels fundamentally about money the same way that I do. Financial stress that arises from differing attitudes can wreak havoc on a marriage, and our shared perspective strengthens us.

A DISCIPLINED APPROACH

Saving through the years is critical to developing the resources for a successful retirement. Most people have heard the common advice that they need to pay themselves first, but it is easier said than done. It can only happen when people live within their means, spending less than they earn over the years. The best advice for making it easier to save is to do so automatically, setting aside a small amount of income regularly.

This disciplined approach could be to build savings for retirement, or it could be to fund a shorter-term goal, even a quite modest one. I recall a time when my parents were talking about buying a television. My father's attitude was that they would get around to it at some point. I suggested that they simply set aside a small amount every month in a jar—an amount that they would not even miss—and before they knew it they would have more than they needed for the purchase. And that's what came to pass. They soon had their new TV, and my mom was all smiles.

On a much larger scale, that's how saving for retirement can work. It should be made as easy as possible. When a couple automatically diverts money from the pay cheque, somehow they don't notice its absence. The accounts still balance, even when they are not spending those funds. If they keep the money in a spending account, however, much of it seems to evaporate.

That practice might seem unworkable as part of the family budget, but by adopting that mentality, people are dedicating themselves to living within their means and establishing priorities. People who have that discipline, and who can think frugally, are the ones who grow their assets. I have known clients with high salaries who have saved very little. Others have modest salaries but have put aside quite a bit over the years.

The most pressing question that potential retirees bring to me is a simple one: Are they in a position that they will not be running out of money? Will their savings fund their lifestyle throughout retirement? In various surveys, the consensus of baby boomers has been that they are more afraid of running out of money than they are of dying. Clearly, it's a huge concern.

That's where Tim Noonan's funded ratio calculator, as he describes in *Someday Rich*, can provide peace of mind. If the calculation shows you to be 100 percent funded, then you will have sufficient income. If it's higher or lower, you can adjust, but either way, you will gain clarity. If you determine that you are on track, then you will not be living with the uncertainty that breeds fears. And if you find that you are fortunate to be overfunded, then you will have more options.

I sometimes discuss this funded ratio calculation along with my goals-based reporting so that my clients can see the bottom line and project where they are headed. Often it helps to ease their worries. The idea is not all to suggest that they should buy an annuity as a guarantee, although that may be a good fit for some. The purpose is to determine whether their resources match up with their needs and goals for retirement. With a good portfolio that provides a consistent income, they can get the reassurance of an annuity without actually having to buy one.

In this era when employer pensions have become far fewer, the retirement goal generally is to build a strong portfolio that can deliver ample and reliable income for a lifetime. Investments typically will be more conservative, to protect all those years of gains, but they also must produce a return that is at least sufficient to keep up with inflation. Whether the retirement "pay cheque" comes from a portfolio or from an annuity, if the annual income stays the same it will command far less purchasing power in twenty years.

IN MY LIFE . . .

GORD AND BERNIE

Living on the hillside of Burnaby, Gord and Bernie realize that it's time to downsize and move somewhere where the going is easier—perhaps to a rancher out in the White Rock area, close to their place in Birch Bay for weekend trips. Gord has been retired for fifteen years, and Bernie for ten. Both worked at Telus, where they met.

Health has become an issue for this couple since Gord had a stroke a few years ago. He has made great progress toward a full recovery through his dedication to regular exercise and a good diet—and the health-conscious Bernie helps to keep him accountable. The stroke was a wake-up call for both of them, and it has led them to put extra emphasis on health matters.

Today, their lifestyle includes workout classes and yoga at the gym. Fitness has always been important to them, but now it has become a passion that they share. You must take time to take care of yourself, they say, as health issues become increasingly important with age. Pay particular attention to the issues that your parents faced, Gord recommends. His father died of colon cancer, so he is diligent about preventive measures and regular screening.

Gord and Bernie enjoy their time together and love to travel, including river cruises in Europe. Family and grandchildren are top of mind for them as they pursue a future of easier living. Retirement, they emphasize, brings the freedom to do what you want—and along with that freedom comes the responsibility to fill that time appropriately. They are careful to keep boundaries and pursue individual interests.

Their advice to other couples is to make sure to do a good job saving for retirement, as it isn't cheap—especially if you like to travel and lead an active life. Saving is particularly important for those who don't have a pension. Before retiring, they say, a couple should prepare themselves for changes to income and expenses.

You may find yourself busier in retirement than you ever imagined, even as you take it at a more leisurely pace. When he retired, Gord made a list of projects that he wanted to do. He's only halfway through that list. He even decided to take on a few jobs as a house painter, and it was fun—for a while. Bernie is so accomplished at yoga that she could be an instructor, but she likewise feels that might take the fun out of it. What is important, they say, is to be open to new opportunities, experiences, and adventures. Keep an open mind, and enjoy these precious years.

STEPS TO A SECURE RETIREMENT INCOME

In planning for a secure retirement income, the first step—and I repeat this because it is so crucial—is to come to a thorough understanding of retirement needs and wants and of the resources that are available to meet them. I work closely with my clients to develop specific objectives and time horizons. Without this step, we cannot determine the right style, type, and balance of investments.

Having attained that clarity, we then do projections of expenses and income, and we look for any gaps. If there are gaps, we need to find a way to cover them. For example, I will work with clients to calculate their pension income, government CPP and OAS, and then see how much of their projected expenses those will cover. Then we determine whether their investments will provide sufficient additional income. Let's say the client has $1 million and is investing at, say, 4 percent net of fees. That will produce $40,000 every year, and if that amount covers the gap, then we can project that the client will be set for retirement and be able to preserve that $1 million principal.

The income plan should divide discretionary and nondiscretionary expenses. The nondiscretionary costs are ones that will be incurred every year, no matter what. These are the essentials, such as food, clothing, and shelter. The discretionary costs are those where the client could cut back—such as forgoing a trip to Hawaii if income is relatively low or expenses are high in a particular year. Retirees need to identify where there is flexibility in the income and spending plan. They do not want to be in a position where they overextend themselves and withdraw excessive money, particularly in a down year for the market. It's hard for a portfolio to recover when a large amount comes out at the same time that the market drops.

That's why major expenses must be projected far into the future. Will the retiree be buying a vacation property in Europe or opening a winery in the Okanagan? If so, those goals must be identified as soon as possible and worked into the retirement income and investment plan. Investments need to be designed appropriately for short-term, mid-term, and long-term goals. A spur-of-the-moment decision to withdraw a large sum has the potential to devastate a portfolio.

When we have made those determinations on goals and time frames, we can assess the level of risk that the retiree is willing or able to accept in the market. This is the point where we can design an investment portfolio to get the job done. The goal is to attain the rate of return needed to achieve those objectives, while reducing the risk as much as possible. We need to find the right balance.

To help assess my clients' risk tolerance, I ask them to answer eleven questions on a "money compass questionnaire." That helps to give them clarity on how much risk they would want to assume, and it also sets expectations for both of us. From there, we set up the appropriate asset allocation, keeping in mind how much risk the portfolio could tolerate and still meet the essentials.

To back up our projections, we use extensive historical data and rely on a professional team of researchers and institutional asset managers to handle the strategic and tactical adjustments going forward. We seek opportunities that can enhance the return without subjecting the portfolio to more risk and volatility. Working with our investment management research (IMR) team, we set up the asset allocations. It's not me alone pushing buttons to buy and sell stocks. This is a structured process of teamwork.

All the while, through all the research and asset selections, we keep in mind the client's overall goals. When we examine performance, cost, volatility, and overall expected return, we are striving for the right balance that will serve the client's stated objectives.

With the investment priorities in place, we then allocate money according to the projected needs and wants. Again, this is an institutional type approach that is highly structured, backed by a large research team, to reduce errors that would take a client off track.

FINDING THE RIGHT ASSET MIX

An effective, visual way to explain allocations is what we call the *bucket system*. Imagine three buckets—one for short-term investing, one for medium term, and one for longer term. Generally, the first bucket would contain cash, for expenses coming up in the next year or two. The second bucket would contain fixed income investments, for expenses coming up in the two or three years beyond that. And the third bucket, for expenses anticipated beyond five years, would contain equities. Basically, the portfolio must include money for short-term spending needs and living expenses, for longer-term needs, and for growth investments to beat inflation.

The asset allocation design seeks to create a blended approach among those three buckets. Overall, it should produce a good mix of returns appropriate for the established level of risk and for the client's income needs. The combination also can result in lower volatility, meaning some of the risks can be offset against others, particularly when we diversify within each of those buckets. The portfolio must include all three of those buckets to create the comprehensive approach needed for a successful retirement.

Here's a look at five types of portfolio that might be appropriate for a particular client's situation and risk tolerance:

Capital Preservation

This portfolio is for investors seeking to avoid risk and volatility and who will accept a return that is lower than average. The aim is to protect principal and also gain some income from safer investments. Much of the portfolio is in fixed income investments, along with some stocks to offset inflation.

Income

The investor accepts modest risk to principal to get a higher yield. The objective is to obtain a dependable income stream, while also seeking to protect principal. Stocks are selected for yield as well as potential for dividend growth to counter inflation.

Income and Growth

The investor is willing to take on risk to achieve growth, while maintaining income. The aim is a balance between bonds, for current income, and stocks, for growth of principal and for dividends. A cross section of stocks seeks to produce income, dividend growth to offset inflation, and capital appreciation to build wealth.

Growth

The investor will accept volatility in the pursuit of above-average returns, with the objective of building wealth over the long term rather than producing current income. The portfolio consists of companies with earnings growth that is consistently above average.

Aggressive Growth

The investor will take on more substantial risk, with more concentrated positions, hoping for higher returns over the long term. Those returns may vary widely from year to year. The aim is higher-than-average growth in capital. The portfolio is heavier on stocks, and current income is not a concern.

The governing principle is this: the sooner you will need the money, the less investment risk you can accept. You can accept more risk for your money if you won't need it for several years. You will be compensated for that additional risk. If you don't need the money for a very long time, then you can take even more investment risk—with the potential for even greater gain.

Many people simply think of risk as the potential for losing money. A lot of advisors will equate risk to volatility measured by standard deviation or how much the portfolio total rises or falls from the average return. But the real risk, as I see it, is not achieving your retirement goals. Goals-based reporting looks at risk from the perspective of whether the client is on track. The biggest risk to retirement security lies in a sudden change in an objective or asset allocation that greatly alters the course of the planning. If an investor is aiming for a specific goal, with a specific timeline, but then changes that timeline and liquidates the money early, trouble could lie ahead.

Let's say you have been investing your money and growing it so that you can retire in ten years. Then you decide to retire tomorrow. Suddenly, you have eliminated that long time horizon. Your portfolio, rather than riding the waves of the market for a decade to produce a more reliable return over time, suddenly is at the mercy of the immediate volatility—and your retirement goals are at stake.

A PORTFOLIO UP TO THE TASK

Spending needs and desires in retirement are a highly personal matter and, of course, will vary greatly from one person to the next. I have many clients who want to do everything they can to help out their children and grandchildren. But is that more of a priority than building a good retirement for themselves? It depends. It's up to the individual.

In any event, these are matters that merit thorough discussion and deep consideration. So many people deplete their retirement funds because of a notion that they should be sending their children to the very best schools. If that is a goal, it should be pursued with great caution. Would it make any sense to spend all your savings to put your children through university, only to put yourself in a position where later on you become financially dependent on them?

As you can see, the previous chapters on setting goals and weighing risks are essential precursors to creating a portfolio that will endure throughout the retirement years. How can people know how much income they will need unless they know what they want to do? Well before retirement, they need to step back and think about what really matters and then begin building toward that end. They should not be depending upon the sale of their house or upon an expected inheritance to fund their retirement. Too often, expectations fall through.

Retirees need a portfolio that is up to the task. They need to embark early on their goals and stick with them. Only then will they be able to develop an income plan that meets their dreams. They should let nothing get in the way of that.

CHAPTER 7

TAKING CARE OF BUSINESS

I met a woman in her seventies whose husband had been dead for a decade, and she still had $800,000 sitting in the business, which wasn't active anymore. She was uncertain what to do about that and how to close down the corporation and pull that money out. Every year she had to deal with her corporate tax return, which isn't cheap and can take a fair bit of work. What she needed was the services of a good accountant and advisor to help make that money productive again and attach it to a goal.

Uncertainty is not uncommon among business owners, and I have found that with my accounting background, I can bring particular value to them—whether they are working to build their base, control taxes, or prepare for an exit so that someone else can run the show. Many business owners, as they consider their own retirement, are really not sure what the next phase should look like. Often they just keep working because that's all they know. And if they have been running a successful business, they quite enjoy it.

It can be tough to contemplate the transition to retirement and the sale of the business. Many business owners make the transition gradually, staying engaged for a while. They take comfort in knowing that they are still contributing, but it is also important to pursue a balanced life with other sources of fulfillment.

As they get closer to retirement, business owners have many questions. Who's going to take over the company? Will it pass to one or more of the children? Will a key employee take over? Will an outside buyer in the same industry purchase the business? What is the best way to approach negotiations with the buyer? What would be the best arrangement from a tax perspective? And just how much is the business worth? Many owners really don't know. Is its value based on the amount of assets, or would an element of goodwill also be involved in the price?

These are fundamental and essential questions, and the transition of the business can be a frustrating process without the right team working together to make it happen.

The sale of a business represents a major shift in the life of the owner and his or her family, and organizing a good team at this time will go far toward a smooth transition into retirement. There is much to consider, and the complications can be numerous. The emotions involved in saying farewell to a life's work can be quite draining in themselves.

THE POWER OF DELEGATING

Business owners are busy people. They have a lot to juggle, and they may lack the time to devote to financial matters. Engineers who are brilliant in their field, for example, might not have the time, inclination, or comprehensive knowledge to invest wisely. I have met so many smart people who nonetheless don't know what to expect in retirement and are unaware of how they can get more of a return than the 1.5 percent of a GIC.

If they are running a business, they might well be better off doing what they do best rather than trying to figure out all the finances on their own. Few people have the depth of understanding required to deal effectively with all the interrelated issues of their financial life. The smart approach, for many, is to delegate the task to an accountant and a planner who can help with the tax management and keep them on track. Successful business owners and CEOs certainly understand the need to surround themselves with other sharp minds with specific areas of expertise. Now, as they retire, they can delegate the financial planning that will see them through the many good years ahead.

Many other business owners are quite capable but concerned about who would handle the financial affairs if they were to pass away early. I have clients who take great comfort in knowing that their spouse would be able to come to me for guidance and that everything would be in order. They also know that, as a younger advisor, I will be there for their children. The continuity is important to them.

It serves the owner well to delegate these matters to specialists with extensive experience in dealing with the many issues surrounding the sale of a business. These involve questions of tax efficiency in structuring the sale and designing a portfolio from the proceeds to produce an adequate income flow for retirement. Comprehensive planning can turn what might have been a disappointing retirement into a fulfilling one.

LONG BEFORE THE SALE

The sale of the business needs to be considered well before it happens. At least five years in advance—longer is better—business owners should develop their exit or succession plan. A lot of them wait until a year or two before retiring, and they often face some surprises and delays as a result.

They may find, for example, that the business is not worth as much as they imagined. Small-business owners sometimes are caught by surprise when they find that their operation is not likely to sell for as much as they thought that it would. A lot of the value of small businesses is associated with the current owner/operator. The owner has developed relationships over the years and may be deeply involved personally in handling the sales and contracts. When that person leaves, the faithful clientele or customers also leave. A small restaurant, for example, may get its customers based on the reputation of the owner, who perhaps is also the talented and creative chef. Potential buyers likely would realize that they would have a hard time retaining those customers with the previous owner out of the picture, and they would be unwilling to pay the price that the seller had anticipated.

If a business owner expects to sell for, say, $5 million and finds out only on the brink of the deal that it's worth half that much, his or her retirement picture can change dramatically. The best approach is to start early and get an accurate valuation and then work out a cash flow that will keep the money working and the income flowing during what could be a long retirement.

INVESTING OUTSIDE THE BUSINESS

I have often worked with retirees who have sold a business and are looking for strategies to invest the proceeds of the sale. However, the business should not have been the sole source of retirement security. To avoid concentrated risk, business owners should be developing other resources along the way. Over-concentration of assets also can be a problem for executives of a company who have a stock option plan. There are ways to reverse some of that risk by reallocating and diversifying.

When much of the owner's wealth is tied up in the business, he or she could face a serious problem if something were to go wrong. Business conditions and economies and technologies can change rapidly and dramatically. Competition can sweep in unexpectedly. Unless the company can adapt, it could be doomed.

To protect against that risk, the owner should have money in investments other than the business itself. This can be quite a change of perspective for business owners, who know how the levers work in their own operation and might feel uncomfortable at the prospect of supplementing their income in another way. Nonetheless, well before the sale they should be diversifying to secure their income and their assets for the long road ahead.

This comes back to the fundamentals that serve everyone well in their financial lives, whether they are running a business or collecting a pay cheque from an employer: pay yourself first, from an early age. Put a priority on developing a secure future. Live within your means. Control spending. Don't be sidetracked by conflicting goals. Make sure you pursue them in the right order. Be certain you have the needed cash flow before buying that dream home in Hawaii with all its related expenses. Ideally, even putting the kids through college should not take priority over a successful retirement.

WHO WILL TAKE THE REINS?

Many owners ponder whether their business should be turned over to family members. If a son or daughter has been deeply involved in it and has proved to be competent, that could be a good choice. But it should never be forced upon anyone. Doing so could endanger the business, particularly if the founding values are not instilled in successive generations. It has been said that the first generation starts a business, the second generation builds the business, and the third generation destroys the business. Certainly there are many exceptions, but the adage is cause for caution.

A business thrives when those who operate it are passionate about it and feel a sense of devotion to its success. If all of the children are off on their own pursuits in life, then it might be best to sell to a key employee or employees who have shown their dedication and loyalty. They might be more motivated for success. Perhaps it would be best to seek an outside buyer in the same industry. The owner needs to keep an open mind for the sake of the business's future.

Thorough planning is important not only in developing an exit strategy but also to provide for a smooth transition in case the owner should pass away sooner than had been anticipated. Business owners should put in place a contingency plan, designed with professional guidance. There are many questions to be considered: Will the ownership be retained by the estate, transferred by sale or gift to family members, or sold to a third party? How would a transfer to family members be done most efficiently? What would be the situation with capital gains or other taxes? If some children are involved in the business and others are not, how will all be treated fairly? Would the sale of the business generate enough income to continue providing for the family? If there is a shortfall, does the owner have life insurance to cover it? How will debts be paid? Those are just some of the questions that arise.

A buy–sell agreement should be drafted to direct the procedures in the event that one partner passes away. Otherwise, that person's spouse could suddenly become the new partner—and that might work out fine, but generally that would not be the most auspicious outcome. The buy–sell agreement will govern what would happen in such a case, specifying, for example, how the surviving partner would buy out the deceased partner's shares. A common solution is life insurance, in which a corporate-owned policy on each partner's life ensures there is enough money in the corporation to complete the buyout—and the proceeds are potentially tax-free. That approach can offer more certainty than self-funding, along with the tax efficiencies.

Similarly, a legal agreement should be drafted to deal with the potential that one of the partners could become disabled. That contingency, too, involves many questions that must be answered in advance. What specifically would constitute a disability? What would be the buyout or succession procedure?

IN MY LIFE . . .
COLIN AND PAT

It has been more than five years since Colin and Pat fully retired from the auto body repair shop where Colin was co-owner and Pat had been an administrator. Over the years, they managed to take a variety of trips together, such as to Palm Springs for golfing, and Colin enjoyed frequent fishing trips. Well respected in the community, the couple continued the good life they long had known as they entered retirement, surrounded by their loving family, including two daughters and four grandchildren.

Colin took an unusual route into retirement, continuing to work doing what he loved until he was nearly seventy—but in the later years he alternated one month on the job with one month off, spending many of the off months in Palm Springs, particularly during the winters. Easing into retirement helped to avoid the surprises that so many retirees face from the sudden change in lifestyle. That was far better, in Colin's view, than just packing up the boxes one day and never returning to the workplace.

It's important to abide by a long-term plan, Colin once told me, praising our longtime relationship as essential to keeping the two of them on track toward their goals. This plan became even more important in their later years as they dealt with more than their share of the unexpected. Colin developed some knee and eye problems, Pat needed a hip replacement, and a few years ago Pat was diagnosed with Alzheimer's. Having a plan and being organized, Colin said, helped the family to handle the stress.

He told me more than once how fortunate he felt that he and Pat were able to enjoy traveling together before their health issues set them back. He went on to reflect on the years since he moved from England to build a life for his family here, saying he was proud of the strong work ethic he had helped instil in his daughters, who have been a tremendous help. He felt content, even as he bravely faced the new challenge of a cancer diagnosis.

Just before Colin passed away in the spring of 2016, he told me that he had found a fullness to his life during retirement, dedicating himself to enjoying his time with his daughters and grandkids, and making sure his beloved wife gets the care she will need long into her future. I am so privileged to have known Colin and helped the two of them over the years—I have learned a great deal from their example.

TAX CONSIDERATIONS

The business owner and his or her advisers also must carefully consider the tax issues involved in the succession plan. Here are just some of those considerations, and they call for due diligence by each party and their teams of tax, legal, and planning professionals:

- Will shares be given to the children?

- How might the capital gains exemption ($824,176 for 2016) be handled, if it is applicable?

- If there are buyouts, will they be via direct sale or share redemptions?

- What might be the tax consequences regarding the receipt of cash from life insurance or disability income?

- Does the executor have the authority to handle all necessary tax matters?

- Has a spousal trust been considered as a means to defer tax at death?

- Is there a strategy for reducing or eliminating probate fees?

- If there are US assets, will the US estate and gift taxes apply in any way?

- Have charitable strategies been considered?

Let's take a brief look at some of the key issues in business transition planning. Whether the transition will be to family members, key employees, or an outside buyer, the goal is to accomplish it with the greatest tax efficiency possible.

Capital Gains

When selling the shares of your corporation, you will have to pay tax on the capital gains, even if you decide to gift your corporation to your kids. The capital gain is the difference between the fair market value and the adjusted cost base. Half of that amount is taxable at your marginal rate.

Lifetime Capital Gains Exemption

The lifetime capital gains exemption may be available to shelter a significant amount of tax on the sale of qualified small-business corporation shares. The 2016 exemption, indexed for inflation, is $824,176 per shareholder. For qualified farming or fishing property, the exemption is $1 million. You can potentially double the exemption if you make your spouse or a family member a shareholder when you set up the corporation. You also will need to take steps to ensure that your company is "pure" for two years before the sale so that it is considered a qualified small-business corporation. This must be done with the guidance of a good accountant.

Estate Freeze

One effective way to gift shares and defer your tax liability is to set up an estate freeze. This transaction lets you "freeze" the value of your current ownership in the corporation so that future growth will accrue to the successor—your son or daughter, for example. Doing so fixes your tax liability at today's value and transfers the tax liability for future growth to the new owners. The freeze often is accomplished by exchanging your common shares for fixed value preferred shares, or "freeze shares." Common shares are then issued to your successor. When you pass away, your preferred shares can be gifted to your children or other successor. In the meantime, you can still maintain voting rights and control of the company with the shares, even as your children are operating it, and your shares can also be producing an income for you. This can be accomplished through an estate freeze and a shareholders agreement. It may also be possible to shelter some or all of the capital gain from the estate freeze using the lifetime capital gains exemption for qualified small-business corporation shares.

Avoiding Double Taxation

If you are transitioning your business within your family, you generally will be selling it rather than gifting shares outright.

After all, this is the money that will be funding your retirement. The sale must be structured carefully, however, because the shares you sell will be considered to be at fair market value. You might wish to give your children a good deal on the shares, but the result could be double taxation. For example, if your business is worth $5 million in fair market value but you decide to sell it to your daughter for $2 million, then you still will be deemed to have sold the shares at their full value. In other words, you will face taxes on a $5 million capital gain (presuming your adjusted cost base is negligible). Meanwhile, your daughter would be starting with a tax base of $2 million, the amount she actually paid. If she decided a month later to sell those shares for their full market value of $5 million, she would face a tax on a $3 million gain.

Receiving Cash or Debt as Proceeds

Receiving cash for the sale is ideal. You get the most options. You can put that money to work to fund your retirement, or you can give some of the proceeds to family members uninvolved in the business transition. However, there can also be an advantage to receiving debt. If you take back debt in the form of a promissory note, you can defer capital gains tax. You can recognize the gain over a period of up to five years. If the sale is to your spouse/partner or to a child or grandchild, you can take the gain over ten years.

Sale to Key Employees

If selling to a family member isn't your primary option, then you may be looking internally within the corporation to set up a manager buyout. The big question is how your employees will be coming up with the financing. This is where debt financing can come into play with the use of a leveraged buyout—essentially, the employees would form a new corporation that would be used to purchase the shares.

Selling to a Third Party

The other most common option, other than selling to family members or internally to current employees, is selling to a third party, such as a supplier, competitor, customer, or a public company. It can be a challenging pursuit, however, and you will do well to work with professionals who have experience in your industry. For assistance, you may wish to be in touch with an investment banker or business broker. You will need a lawyer to properly structure the sale and minimize liabilities, an accountant to help manage taxes, and a financial advisor who has experience working with retirees.

Sale of Assets

From a tax perspective, a main planning point is how the purchase price of the assets will be allocated. The seller generally will want to allocate the purchase price to assets that, when sold, give rise to capital gains, such as land. The buyer generally will want to assign the purchase price to depreciable assets that can be fully written off in future years. If the business is sold for more than the value of the tangible assets—the buildings, inventory, equipment, etc.—then the amount exceeding the fair market value of those hard assets is referred to as "goodwill."

The Role of Life Insurance

The use of life insurance can play an important role in transition planning, especially if there is an immediate need for cash liquidity, such as when a shareholder dies. The tax-free death benefit from life insurance can be an effective means of buying out the value of that person's shares, as provided in a shareholder agreement. It is important that the agreement define "value" as not including the value of the life insurance itself. Also, make sure that your business is a qualified small-business corporation so that part or all of the lifetime capital gains exemption can be used.

CLEANING UP FOR THE SALE

Well before the sale, the owner should be thinking about cleaning up the business—both physically and financially—to get the best possible sales price. The more that the owner can streamline and restructure the business in advance, the more valuable it will be to someone else.

A buyer will pay more for a company that will generate a profit readily. Establishing that profitability—particularly if those profits still are on the rise—likely will make potential buyers agree to pay significantly more. Well before the sale, the business owner should seek ways to cut costs and run the operation more efficiently. For several years before selling, the owner should strive to consistently boost revenue and sales and be able to show a track record of profitability. A buyer will be looking for consistent cash flow from the start, so try to enhance recurring sources of revenue that will be valuable to a new owner immediately. Be able to produce reliable contracts with customers and vendors. Finalize leases and other agreements.

Buyers are looking for reassurance that the business will be able to thrive when the seller is out of the picture. They will be looking to see that the company has documented procedures and processes in place that allow it to run smoothly even when the seller is no longer directly involved. A lot of small-business owners have trouble taking vacations because they fear the place will go south when they are gone. That is not the impression to give to potential buyers.

A buyer will also be concerned about losing too many of the employees currently on staff. By building an excellent and loyal workforce that is committed to staying, the owner can provide that reassurance and effectively increase the value of the company. A way to build that kind of motivated workforce is to provide key employees with long-term incentives, such as vested ownership in equity and bonuses linked to profits.

The owner should think like the buyer. What makes the company special? What services or products differentiate it? What is its edge over the competition? With those questions in mind, the owner should be promoting and enhancing those features well before the sale.

It should go without saying, but when you are selling your business, it should be looking good. A new coat of paint can go a long way, as well as renovations and updated accouterments. In other words, pay attention to the curb appeal. Keep the floors swept, the windows washed, and the restrooms smelling sweet. First impressions last. Just as you need to clean up the books, so you also need to clean up the premises.

When preparing to sell, I suggest that business owners keep the following in mind as a checklist:

- Make sure to do that cleanup on all aspects of the business, and be prepared to continue running it as long as necessary.

- Get a clear idea of the business's value, based on appraisals and industry standards. Do not overprice it, and always consider the point of view of the buyer.

- Develop a professional team with a strong network that includes expertise in accounting and legal issues.

- Work with a trusted business broker who specializes in the industry and can find qualified potential buyers.

- Consider key employees, an employee-owned ESOP, or competitors as possible buyers.

- Be able to produce at least two years of records that have been audited and to provide full documentation.

- In cases of seller financing, be sure to qualify the buyer. Don't expect to be paid in cash.

- Seek out tax advice every step of the way.

VALUING A BUSINESS

There are numerous ways that a business can be valued—multiples of revenue, for example, or calculations involving cash flow—and the method used will depend on the industry. First, take a look at how competitors are valuing their businesses or how other businesses in the industry did their valuations when they were sold. It is best to use a professional independent business valuator, especially if selling to children or other family members, because of the need to avoid the potential for double taxation.

Here are some common methods:

Asset-Based

This could be the book value, which is the company's net worth in assets minus liabilities as shown in the financial statements. Or this could be the liquidation value, which assumes that the business sells all its assets, pays off all its debts including taxes, and distributes the surplus to its shareholders.

Earnings and Cash Flow

This could be a calculation of discounted cash flow, in which value is based on the future cash flows of the business. Or the calculation might be going-concern value, which assumes that the business will continue operating and compares the current cash flows with future inflows to make projections.

Sometimes a buyer can see a value in creating economies of scale and will pay a premium. Experienced business brokers or accountants will understand the details. It is important to find someone who is familiar with your particular industry.

A MATTER OF PRIDE

In all cases, starting early is wise. Parents and children should be thinking years ahead about whether there is a potential for succession within the family. When I took over my father's business, we both felt a great sense of pride that the business would be continuing in the family, and I am particularly grateful to be serving clients today who were with my dad for decades. Not only do I feel that pride but I also feel quite accountable to him, as well as to my clients, to do my very best. This was a business that he built, and I feel driven to live up to his reputation.

I like to shop at a popular men's clothing store called Grasbys, where I truly get a feel for that sense of family pride. Three generations work there, sometimes all on the same day: the father, Frank, his son Jason, and his grandson Brandon. They must feel quite a sense of accomplishment and satisfaction when they look around and see what they have built together.

You can sense it when you walk in the doors: this is a family that treats you as family. That, I believe, is the foundation of business success, and that is the spirit that I wish to bring to the financial planning practice that I am honoured to continue in my father's footsteps.

CHAPTER 8

SECURING YOUR LEGACY

When I was fifteen years old, a friend and I went off for a day of skiing and snowboarding on Cypress Mountain in Vancouver. It was a beautiful day with plenty of fresh powder, and as the hour approached when my friend's parents were to pick us up, we decided to sneak in one more run.

That morning, my mother's parting words to me had been: "Make sure you don't go out of bounds!" I scarcely heard her. "Sure, Mom," I said as I ran out the door. But during that final run, as we made our way just outside the boundary ropes to get to the freshest powder, we became disoriented. We kept cutting farther and farther to the right, thinking that would get us closer to the main run, but we ended up in a gully with so much powder that we couldn't hike back out. There clearly had been avalanches there.

Eventually, the gully turned into a creek with a waterfall. Soaking wet, we wandered along the ravines, still hoping beyond hope that we might make it to the parking lot at the base. With darkness falling, we realized we weren't going to make it out, and so we hunkered down on our snowboards, wet and shivering in the icy air. Hypothermia was setting in.

The hours passed. Then far in the distance we heard a search and rescue team sounding its horn, and we called out that we were there—and after what seemed like hours longer of sirens and shouts, the rescuers found us. As it turned out, we were quite far from the main parking lot at the base, and when we eventually hiked out with the rescue team we were all the way at the base of Grouse Mountain, near the Capilano water reservoir. The rescuers had discovered our tracks where we first went out of bounds, and they deduced where we had likely headed. People get lost in that same "Australian gully" every year, and many have died. The men risked their own lives to save ours.

The hike back out was almost as dangerous. The sun was rising as we emerged from the wilderness and into the arms of our parents, who were as relieved as we were. My friend's mother, who had arrived the previous evening to pick us up, had become alarmed as the mountain cleared of skiers and our backpacks were the only ones left at the lodge.

A couple weeks later, my friend and I returned to the slopes where we had nearly perished—and this time, we were there to promote mountain safety. We met with the rescuers who had found us. The *Vancouver Sun* ran the story of our ordeal on the front page, and we were able to warn others of the enticement and danger of going out of bounds. In search of something better and exciting, we had found ourselves getting in deep, but by the time we recognized the risk it was too late to make it back to safety. Instead, we took a direction that put us in far greater peril, and we were at the mercy of the elements.

As I think about it now, that's what happens to a lot of investors—although I certainly wasn't pondering the stock market that night on the mountain. Something did change inside of me that night, however. It was a turning point where I began to set goals for myself. I began striving for success.

In the years ahead, those aspirations were in part athletic: I became captain of the high school rugby team and experienced trips to Australia and Fiji, to Argentina and Uruguay. I played varsity rugby at university and went to trials for the Canadian U-21 World Cup Squad. In part, my goals were academic: I got my bachelor's of commerce degree in entrepreneurship at UVic and later attained my CA, CFP®, and CIM designations and licensing for securities and insurance. And in part, my ambitions were career-oriented: I worked at a public account-ing firm, became an entrepreneur with Navigate Apparel, and took over my father's financial planning business.

"Striving for success," however, has meant more to me than reaching for athletic and financial and career goals. I under-stood, after that brush with death on the mountain, that life was more than about myself; there was something bigger out there. Sometimes it takes quite a scare before people start pondering their legacy. As I huddled on my snowboard through that frigid night, I had felt stupid and selfish. I resolved that, if I made it out of that mess, I would appreciate my family more and would make it up to them for what I had put them through. I would focus on what really mattered. I would give back more than I took from life.

I believe that each of us must take that next step of giving back. How can we reach out to others? Which charities might we support with our time or resources? Those are the questions we should be asking ourselves. That is the spirit that has driven me to teach financial literacy to children through the CPA volunteer program. That is why I wrote that *Pogo Pig* book for children on goal setting. That is why I volunteer as the treasurer on the board of one of the largest charities in town called Sources. I have been involved in a variety of charitable and community efforts. Much has been given to me, and I believe that I should give of myself in return.

HIERARCHY OF PRIORITIES

I work with many clients who have more money than they will ever spend. That provides them with opportunities to live even more purposefully through charitable giving or setting up a foundation, and I gain satisfaction in helping them to figure out how to reach their goals. The first step is to make sure that they are taking care of their financial planning with the appropriate priorities.

This chart shows the hierarchy of a couple's planning needs. At the base is *personal financial independence*, and that must be funded first. That is the foundation, and it should be set in place before building further up the pyramid.

HIERARCHY OF PLANNING NEEDS

This pyramid shows how prudent planning starts with a strong foundation and builds its way up. Although one need may be more exciting to talk about than the others, the order of planning for them is extremely important for long-term success.

Many people want to build their *family legacy* and help their children and grandchildren. However, they should not put so much attention on assisting their children that it is to the detriment of their own needs. That's too much of a sacrifice. In fact, a couple will find it easier to help when they themselves are financially stable. They must find the optimal balance. Many couples believe, with good reason, that they should be careful about giving too much money to their children. It could harm them to get an easy ride.

Once the couple feels that they have taken care of themselves and have assisted other family members appropriately, they likely will reach the point of wondering, "What else is there?" That is when many people's thoughts turn to *social legacy* and the charities that they might want to support. They look for a cause or institution to which they can relate—one that has been meaningful to them through the years or that they believe serves a worthy purpose. Some people may wonder why this is so important. A 2008 Harvard study has shown giving money to someone else lifted participant's happiness more than spending it on themselves (known as "helpers high"). As well, a 1999 study out of Berkeley found that elderly people who volunteered for two or more organizations were 44 percent less likely to die over the next five years than were non-volunteers. I believe giving back to important causes should be done throughout everyone's lifetime, whether it's volunteering time or donating money, especially if you have a strong connection to the social program. Charity and volunteering benefit those who receive as well as those who give.

During a recent review of a client's estate planning document we created, the client, Rita, looked at me and said, "If Freddy only knew how much money we had amassed over our lifetime." Rita's husband had developed Alzheimer's and was in a care home with a condition that was worsening by the week. After further discussion Rita expressed how much it would mean to give back to a charity that did research for Alzheimer's—so people wouldn't have to go through what Freddy was going through. After carefully assessing their personal financial health and their family wishes, we focused on what really made Rita excited—the legacy that would be left behind when Freddy passed away. Tears of sadness soon turned to tears of joy as we embarked on planning for Rita and Freddy's new legacy.

Charitable giving can be done directly, but often it is accomplished by setting up a family foundation that can endure as a legacy beyond the donor's lifetime. Because of the work involved in establishing a foundation, as well as the associated fees, it makes more sense when the contributions to fund the foundation will be over $3 million.

A donor-advised fund is an efficient alternative to a foundation with a much lower initial contribution. They can be setup with an investment advisor with as little as a $25,000 contribution and, like a foundation, it will carry your legacy beyond your years. Those assets grow tax-free within the fund, which means more money will be available for the charities. The donor gets a receipt for the value of the donations, which can be used as an immediate tax credit; there's no need to wait until the donations actually are distributed. Meanwhile, the family selects the specific charities to support and could choose different ones each year. The family gets regular reports on the activities and current value of the fund, and all the contributions to a variety of charities are tracked in one convenient statement.

IN MY LIFE . . .
MEIRIC AND KATHY

Recently retired and preparing for a four-month tour of North America in their truck and fifth-wheel trailer, Meiric and Kathy couldn't be more excited about the balance they have found in retirement.

That does not mean work is over for Meiric—far from it! As an award-winning engineer, Meiric has impacted most major rapid transit projects in the Lower Mainland over the last thirty years, including the Canada and Evergreen Lines. A lifelong worker, Meiric is happy to continue building his legacy part time by continuing the engineering and teaching that he loves so much, while still traveling and spending time with Kathy and their children, three granddaughters, and twenty-four-pound labradoodle.

For Meiric, as he tells me, his true legacy is education: by funding a Registered Education Savings Plan (RESP) to help with their granddaughters' educational needs and by mentoring young people through work and through his teachings at UBC and BCIT. It is the main reason Meiric has decided to continue working part time, a move Kathy fully supports, even though they are financially prepared for retirement. She is enjoying her transition and is looking forward to their future, wherever the road takes them.

Meiric and Kathy are a true example of living retirement by the same rules that they lived their working days: working hard, planning ahead, following their passion, and mixing in some travel every chance they get.

EXPLORING THE POSSIBILITIES

Most people want to leave some sort of legacy, but they often don't know how it would be possible. They may be concerned that donating to charity would shortchange their children or other family members who are expecting a larger inheritance. A couple might feel that every dollar going to charity would be a dollar less for their loved ones—but that need not be so. They should discuss these matters with their children. They well might find out that the children do not need or expect a big inheritance. An open dialogue is essential.

In many situations, through proper planning, people can do more for both their families and charity while saving on taxes. Instead of the government collecting a major share and distributing the assets as it sees fit, they could keep control over exactly who benefits from their life's work.

Although donations are just one way to support charities— the volunteering of time is an essential way to give back, too— there are significant tax incentives to providing monetary gifts. For the first $200 of donations every year, you get a 15 percent federal tax credit. Any donations beyond that amount, however, get a 29 percent federal tax credit. Each of the provinces also offers its own additional credits.

You can donate as much as 75 percent of your net income in a year, and you can combine up to five years of smaller donations to get past the $200 threshold so that you can get the higher credit. Spouses also can combine their donations on one return, and a donation made by either of them can be split between both of them in any proportion for tax purposes. First-time donors also can claim a "super credit" of an additional 25 percent on cash contributions up to $1,000.

You are not limited to cash for your donations. For example, some people may wish to donate real estate or even artwork—and the tax credit on those generally would be calculated on their fair market value. That can be an advantageous approach because it allows people to contribute to charity without having to go to the trouble of actually selling the property. Some people choose to donate stocks that have significantly appreciated. They get a tax credit on the full value of the shares, but they are not taxed on the capital gain.

LIFE INSURANCE IN ESTATE PLANNING

Life insurance often plays a key role in estate and legacy planning strategies. Life insurance policies often are among assets donated to charity, for example. Generally, the amount of the gift is considered to be equal to the cash surrender value of the policy. Or a charity might be named as beneficiary, thereby providing the estate with a tax credit based on the amount payable.

A traditional role of life insurance is to take care of dependents—and these days, when young people are staying at home longer, many retirees still do feel that need. Many retirees married later in life, and they may also have stepchildren from second marriages. Life insurance provides a way to leave a larger estate to those beneficiaries.

It can also be a tax efficient means of "equalizing" an estate. For example, if you operate a business but only one of your two children wants to take it over, how can you accomplish that transition in fairness to both? Or if you have helped out one of your children significantly more than the other—assisting with the purchase of a house, for example—what will you be able to do for the other to show equal treatment? A good solution could be an insurance policy naming that other child as the beneficiary.

Life insurance can provide coverage for outstanding taxes, debts, or other obligations due when the policyholder passes away. A vacation property, for example, could be subject to significant taxes, and the heirs who receive it might not have the money to pay that amount. With a permanent life insurance policy in place, however, the proceeds can be paid out tax-free to cover that liability. Also, as I pointed out in the last chapter, life insurance is an efficient means of funding a buy–sell agreement for the transition of a business. It can provide the means to buy out the business interests of a partner who has passed away.

Many retirees want to know that their loved ones will not be burdened with the cost of paying for their funeral and final expenses. That, too, can be a function of life insurance—a much more modest expense to cover but one that can bring significant peace of mind. It's comforting to know that your loved ones will not have to fuss with the finances in their time of grief.

ESSENTIAL ESTATE DOCUMENTS

Everyone has an estate plan by default. It's the government's plan—but it very likely wouldn't be the one that people would choose for themselves. The government's plan works slowly, and it can be quite costly. Let's take a look at some of the steps you can take to avoid that frustration and to help plan efficiently for a lasting legacy.

Far too many people put off the drafting of their will, which directs where their assets will go when they die. Not only should everyone have one, but they should also review it every three to five years and whenever there has been a significant life change. This is a basic document that is a fundamental part of estate planning.

Many people will also set up a trust to more specifically govern the disposition of assets over the long term, with control continuing even after death. A trust can include a wide variety of provisions, including, for example, arrangements for children with special needs and limitations to prevent wasteful spending by an heir.

Trusts offer some tax advantages and can also protect assets from lawsuits, creditors, and divorce claims. They can cost some money to set up, but they can also prevent the costs of the government probate process. In British Columbia, the probate cost is 1.4 percent on amounts over $50,000 (0.6 percent for amounts between $25,000 and $50,000), calculated on the value of the estate situated in British Columbia. That adds up quickly, though proper planning can go far toward reducing that cost.

You should also plan for incapacity, and consider setting up powers of attorney for financial affairs and representation agreements for health care. Someone must have the authority to make essential decisions if you are incapacitated. A health-care directive, or living will, is another important document. It allows you to record your wishes on end-of-life issues, such as life support and resuscitation.

Someone should be named as executor of the estate, and if you have a trust, you must designate a trustee. Whoever is given that responsibility should first consent, of course, and you should have a thorough conversation about the matter. I like to talk with the executor in a family meeting long before anything happens so that we can make sure we all are on the same page. The responsibility of executors can be arduous, and therefore such advance consultation can help greatly. We look to make sure that taxes, expenses, and debts all have been addressed, either self-funded or perhaps through an insurance policy.

FOR THE RECORD

As part of my estate planning services for clients, I provide them with a record-keeper document, on which they can write down important information that their executor and loved ones will be able to find in one convenient place. Most of the information that the record keeper tracks is financial in nature, and it is meant to be used in the event that the client passes on or becomes incapacitated. The record keeper goes a long way toward easing retirees' commonly expressed worry that they might become a burden to others.

I recommend that my clients review the document at least once a year, updating it as necessary. It should be kept in a secure location, such as a safe or safety deposit box, and they can keep an electronic copy as well. They may also wish to send a copy to their executor for safekeeping.

The record keeper tracks a long list of essential information. Everything that the client owns, including investments and real estate, is listed, as well as any debts or other obligations and the numbers of all credit cards. It lists banks and financial institutions; trusts and other estate planning documents; and the locations of important documents, safety deposit boxes, keys, and more. It even details any funeral arrangements that have been made. To receive a free copy of the estate planning record keeper, visit www.bryansommer.com.

The intent of the record keeper is to save loved ones a lot of time and frustration—and potentially a lot of money. And that, actually, is the overall purpose of estate planning. When the time has come to move on from this life, you want to be certain that you have done all you can to secure an enduring legacy. This is not a matter strictly of money. You are passing on your values, your ethics, and the story of who you were and what you believed. That is the bequest that matters. How you manage your money is just part of the larger picture of how you manage your life.

ONWARD TO ABUNDANCE

In my university days, I had a humbling experience that rein-forced some major life lessons. It was not as extreme as my brush with death on the mountain when I was a teenager, but it did help to set my course.

I had long loved rugby and did well at the sport in high school and university, but I had suffered a series of injuries that kept me from trying out for the rep teams, including the U-19 Canadian national team. Now, at the University of Victoria, one of the top rugby schools in the country at the time, I had another chance to try out for the honour of representing Canada at the U-21 Rugby World Cup in England. However, doing so would be in conflict with another opportunity that summer—to travel as part of an exchange program at the business school. I dearly loved to travel, as I still do.

Something had to give, and so I chose to participate in the rugby tryout, passing up the international exchange opportu-nity. I attended the camp and proceeded to sprain my ankle halfway through the tryout. I didn't make the team. I would not be going to England. I felt devastated. I had sacrificed so much and put so much effort into preparation and fund raising. I had wanted so badly, both in high school and university, to represent my country. Would I have nothing to show for it?

I was down, but I was not out. I thought back to that night on the mountain. I knew that I could persevere in the face of difficulty. The next year, in playing varsity rugby back at the University of Victoria, I was named the most improved player and won the Graham Clark Scholarship recognizing dedication and commitment to the game and a solid work ethic. I had come through, and I felt honoured by the distinction. It was yet another reminder that humility can lead to success.

I can see now that difficulties have been part of what has shaped me. I value my strong family background and academic opportunities, but we also build character by overcoming obstacles. One must remain always humble, and that is the way that I want to live my life. That is the spirit within people that motivates them to reach out to others.

The desire to give back should be part of a well-balanced retirement and of life in general. Not only does it do your own heart good, by building a sense of self-worth that sometimes goes missing in the retirement years, but it also serves as an inspiration to the children and grandchildren who will carry on your legacy.

Each of us should lead by example. That's a lesson that I have taken from the world of sports and that I look to exhibit daily in my relationships. I strive to truly get to know people, and that depth of understanding is the best way that I can help my clients. By sharing the expertise that I have gained in my education, career, and life itself, I can help them to thrive.

Because I care about them, I can give them the best of care. In that way, too, I feel that I am giving back.

If you plan carefully and dedicate yourself to improving and succeeding, then you can do far more than making sure that you won't run out of money. You can enjoy an abundant retirement that is better than you ever imagined. This is supposed to be the best time of life, the fulfillment of your years of hard work.

Certainly it's not all butterflies and rainbows. Retirement has its share of stresses. A study by the Institute of Economic Affairs found that retirement increases the probability of suffering from clinical depression by about 40 percent. In any life, troubles are likely to come around. Life, however, is not about lying low to get through the storm. It is about learning to dance in the rain. The more you give back, the more you will get back.

The retirement years are the big reveal of life. When you cross that line, you gain some of the deepest perspectives on what it's all about. With the right spirit and diligent preparation, you can set your own agenda and live your dreams. Exciting times lie ahead, and I am privileged to serve as your guide.

APPENDIX I: FINANCIAL VISION

The following is a sample Financial Vision document we would create for a client.

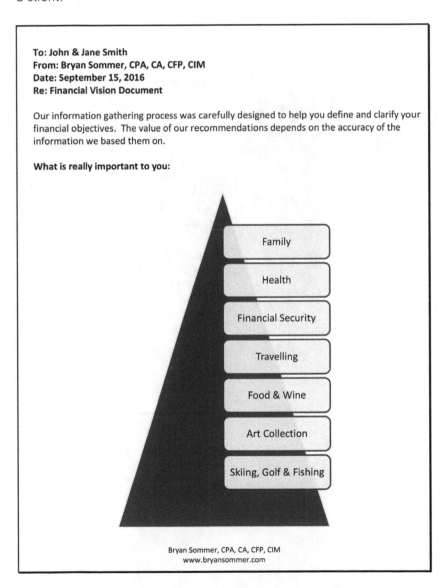

To: John & Jane Smith
From: Bryan Sommer, CPA, CA, CFP, CIM
Date: September 15, 2016
Re: Financial Vision Document

Our information gathering process was carefully designed to help you define and clarify your financial objectives. The value of our recommendations depends on the accuracy of the information we based them on.

What is really important to you:

Family

Health

Financial Security

Travelling

Food & Wine

Art Collection

Skiing, Golf & Fishing

Bryan Sommer, CPA, CA, CFP, CIM
www.bryansommer.com

Where are you today?

Cash Reserves	Debt	Growth/Income	Insurance
Now:	Now:	Now:	Now:
$100K	$0	$750K RRSP's	$2M UL Policy
		$140K TFSA's	
		$1M Non-Reg	
		$4M Holdco	

		$5.89M	
Future:	Future:	Future:	Future:
$100K	$0	$10M with	$4M UL Policy
		$150K annual	
		income	

Bryan Sommer, CPA, CA, CFP, CIM
www.bryansommer.com

Your Planning Objectives

Listed below are the top planning objectives you identified as being important (What objectives do you have that take time, money and planning?):

Objective #1

- **To have consistent and reliable income in retirement.**

- Amount: $150K per year

- Date: Now

- Why/Feeling: So we don't have to worry about money and we can focus on the things we really enjoy like family and travelling.

Objective #2

- **To reduce the amount of taxes we pay.**

- Amount: as much as possible

- Date: Now

- Why/Feeling: So we have more net income in our pockets.

Objective #3

- **To grow our estate and provide a buffer while we are alive.**

- Amount: $10M

- Date: By the time we reach age 80

- Why/Feeling: So we can put half in our foundation focused on mental health and give the other half to our three kids.

Bryan Sommer, CPA, CA, CFP, CIM
www.bryansommer.com

APPENDIX II: GOALS-BASED REPORTING

The following is a sample Goals-Based Reporting document we would create for a client.

CLIENT OBJECTIVE

To have consistent tax efficient income in retirement while growing our estate.

INPUTS AND ASSUMPTIONS

GOAL: Your primary goal is to withdraw amounts per the schedule on the following page as well as to leave $10,000,000 at age 80.

HORIZON: The investment horizon for your goal is 20 years.

ANNUAL RETURN ASSUMPTION: Your financial professional assumes an Annual Return of 4%.

CONTROL LIMIT: The upper and lower control limits set by your financial advisor are 20% and 20% respectively.

CONTRIBUTION AND DISTRIBUTION ASSUMPTIONS

The Goals-based illustration takes into account the following contribution and distribution assumptions during the accumulation period.

Year	Distributions	Contributions	Age
<1	$150,000	$0	60
1	$150,000	$0	61
2	$150,000	$0	62
3	$150,000	$0	63
4	$150,000	$0	64
5	$150,000	$0	65
6	$150,000	$0	66
7	$150,000	$0	67
8	$150,000	$0	68
9	$150,000	$0	69
10	$150,000	$0	70
11	$150,000	$0	71
12	$150,000	$0	72
13	$150,000	$0	73
14	$150,000	$0	74
15	$150,000	$0	75
16	$150,000	$0	76
17	$150,000	$0	77
18	$150,000	$0	78
19	$150,000	$0	79
20	$150,000	$0	80

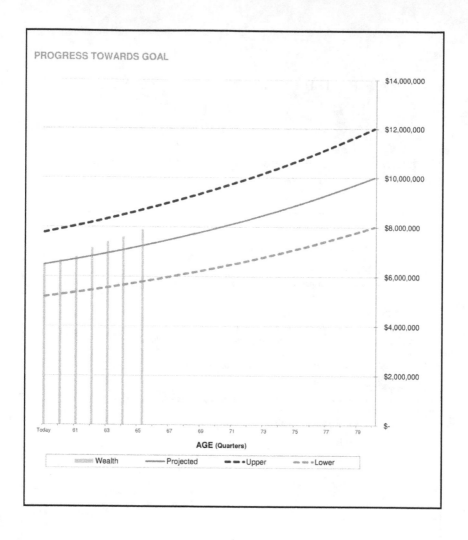

PROGRESS TOWARDS GOAL

APPENDIX III: ROADMAP

The following is a sample Roadmap document we would create for a client.

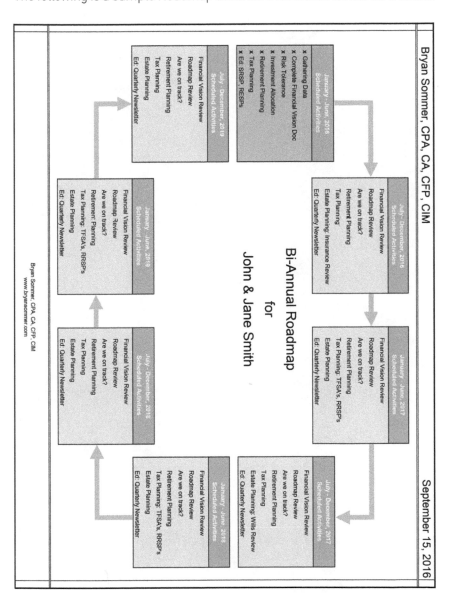

JAMIE GOLOMBEK'S TAX TIPS

It's important for clients to review their overall tax planning strategy with a tax professional to make the most of any opportunities available, especially as a result of new savings and investment vehicles, credits and tax policy changes that come into effect each year. Here is a list of tax-saving opportunities of which your clients should be aware:

1. **Tax-loss selling**: Tax-loss selling is the practice of selling investments that are in an accrued loss position in order to offset capital gains realized either in the current year or in the previous three years. For securities denominated in a foreign currency, be aware that currency fluctuations can affect the capital gain or loss that is reported.

2. **RRSP annuitants who turn seventy-one**: Seniors turning seventy-one during the year only have until December 31 rather than the normal sixty days following the calendar year to make their final Registered Retirement Savings Plan (RRSP) contribution before converting the plan into a Registered Retirement Income Fund (RRIF) or purchasing an annuity.

3. **Contribute to an RESP**: Registered Education Savings Plans (RESPs) offer an opportunity for tax-deferred (or, in many cases, potentially tax-free)

education savings and the prospect of supplementing savings with a number of government grants, most significantly, the Canada Education Savings Grants of $500 annually, up to a maximum of $7,200 per child.

4. **Review RRIF withdrawals**: The RRIF minimum withdrawal factors were decreased in 2015. A client who withdrew more than the new minimum amount in 2015 will be permitted to re-contribute any excess (up to the old minimum amount) until February 29, 2016, and the amount re-contributed will be tax deductible in 2015.

5. **Make a donation**: When clients make a donation to a registered charity or foundation, they will be entitled to a donation tax credit for the amount given. By gifting publicly traded securities, including mutual funds, donors not only receive a tax receipt for the fair market value of the securities being donated but any capital gains taxes are eliminated. Pooling donations with a spouse or partner such that the total is over the $200 threshold can also help to receive a higher donation credit.

6. **Contribute to an RDSP**: Canadians eligible for the Disability Tax Credit, their parents and other eligible contributors can contribute to a Registered Disability Savings Plan (RDSP) and apply for up to $70,000 in matching Canada Disability Savings Grants (CDSGs) and up to $20,000 of income-tested Canada Disability Savings Bonds (CDSBs).

7. **Income splitting**: For clients who are in a high tax bracket, it might be beneficial to have some investment income taxed in the hands of family members (such as a spouse, common-law partner, or children) who are in a lower tax bracket. To avoid attribution, clients can lend funds to family members, provided the rate of interest on the loan is at least equal to the government's prescribed rate, which is 1 percent until at least March 31, 2016.

8. **Split that pension**: Canadians may split up to half of their pension income with their spouse or common-law partner. Aside from the benefit of reducing taxes, one may also be able to preserve some or all of the age credit and avoid or minimize the Old Age Security benefits "clawback."

9. **Deduct investment expenses**: Interest paid on money borrowed for investment purposes, as well as investment counseling fees for non registered accounts, are tax deductible as a carrying charge on Schedule 4 of the federal personal tax return.

10. **Apply now to pay less tax all year**: Clients may reduce tax deductions at source by completing CRA Form T1213 (Quebec taxpayers must also complete Form TP-1016-V) to receive a refund throughout the entire year.

ABOUT THE AUTHOR

Proudly carrying on the family tradition within the financial services industry, Bryan Sommer is an investment advisor and portfolio manager with CIBC Wood Gundy. With over ten years of experience as a professional accountant and investment advisor, Bryan is well versed in assisting clients with their tax, investment, retirement, and estate planning needs and holds designations as a Chartered Professional Accountant (CPA, CA), Certified Financial Planner™ (CFP®), and Chartered Investment Manager (CIM®). Bryan obtained his business degree with a concentration in entrepreneurship from the University of Victoria.

Bryan works closely with individuals and families to create a holistic financial plan to build, preserve, and transition their wealth according to their priorities. He believes that a thorough financial plan starts with an understanding of the family's values, beliefs, and goals, and he supports them with a plan that points the way for future years and across future generations. Together with his team, he provides clients access to a comprehensive range of products and services, including tax planning, charitable giving, business succession planning, professional investment management, retirement planning, and estate planning.

Born and raised in White Rock/South Surrey, Bryan is dedicated to helping his community. This is demonstrated by his involvement as an area leader with CPA Canada's Financial

Literacy program and as a board of director and treasurer for Sources Community Resource Centres. The local newspaper, *The Now Newspaper*, also listed him as best financial planner in 2013, and he was voted the top financial advisor in the Reader's Choice Awards 2016 Best of the Peninsula Peace Arch News Awards. Outside of work and volunteering, Bryan enjoys spending time with his wife and daughter, skiing, golfing, playing tennis, and traveling the world.

Printed in the USA
CPSIA information can be obtained
at www.ICGtesting.com
JSHW012052140824
68134JS00035B/3402

9 781599 327440